Singing Bel Canto

Singing Bel Canto
Art & Science

An introduction to the art of beautiful singing based on the Bel Canto traditions

Michelle Nova
Patricia Collins

This edition first published 2014 © 2014 by Compton Publishing Ltd.

Registered office: Compton Publishing Ltd, 30 St. Giles', Oxford, OX1 3LE, UK Registered company number: 07831037

Editorial offices: 3 Wrafton Road, Braunton, Devon, EX33 2BT, UK

Web: www.comptonpublishing.co.uk

The right of the author to be identified as the author of this work has been asserted in accordance with the UK Copyright, Designs and Patents Act 1988.

All rights reserved. No part of this publication may be reproduced, stored in a retrieval system, or transmitted, in any form or by any means, electronic, mechanical, photocopying, recording or otherwise, except as permitted by the UK Copyright, Designs and Patents Act 1988, without the prior permission of the publisher.

Trademarks: Designations used by companies to distinguish their products are often claimed as trademarks. Any brand names and product names used in this book are trade names, service marks, trademarks or registered trademarks of their respective owners. The publisher is not associated with any product or vendor mentioned in this book.

Permissions: Where necessary, the publisher and author(s) have made every attempt to contact copyright owners and clear permissions for copyrighted materials. In the event that this has not been possible, the publisher invites the copyright owner to contact them so that the necessary acknowledgments can be made.

ISBN 978-1-909082-12-0

A catalogue record for this book is available from the British Library.

Cover image: La Nova Singers (www.lanovastudios.co.uk) in performance, by kind permission of Christchurch Priory, Dorset. UK.

Cover photograph: Lemonade Pictures, www.lemonadepictures.co.uk.

Cover design: David Siddall, www.davidsiddall.com

Illustrations: Ethan Danielson

Set in Adobe Caslon Pro 12pt by Stuart Brown

1   2014

Table of Contents

Acknowledgements	vii
Preface	ix
Chapter 1: Origins of Bel Canto	1
Chapter 2: Vocal anatomy and applying Bel Canto technique	9
Chapter 3: Singing sounds	37
Chapter 4: Understanding how to sing a song	47
Chapter 5: Example songs	55
Chapter 6: Prepare to sing	59
Chapter 7: Learning to sing	69
Appendix I	71
Appendix II	73
Glossary	75
References	81
Index	83

Acknowledgements

Our families, fellow singers and those we have taught have given great support to the development of this book. A few people deserve our especial thanks:

Ethan Danielson, for his work in translating our diagrams into such beautiful illustrations. Nigel Nother, Michelle's husband, has supported her and La Nova singers for many years; his dedication has permitted Michelle to achieve so much. All of the students who have successfully learnt the Bel Canto technique have honed Michelle's skill of teaching this method and demonstrated its beauty; Michelle's singing teacher, Antonio Manzoni, deserves great praise for his endless encouragement, inspiration and lifelong promotion of Bel Canto as a singing method.

To past and future pupils

Preface

The aim of this book is to give an explanation of the Bel Canto technique and how it has developed over time, an accurate description of the anatomical structures used when singing in this technique combined with a way of visualising these structures, and a practical method for the production of the singing voice. The intention is to give an insight into the basic understanding of this method and the realisation that it is for *all* singers, not just classical.

The exact meaning of words and phrases changes over the years and what one generation means or signifies by any term or phrase changes and means something subtly or completely different to the next generation. For this reason the present day meaning of the main terms used in this description of Bel Canto singing are defined. When learning to sing, a whole philosophy of historical interpretation and beliefs are also implicitly transferred between teacher and pupil. It is hoped this text presents a clear view of the process and technique of singing and makes all the information presented explicit.

Chapter 1
Origins of Bel Canto

The words Bel Canto literally mean 'Beautiful Singing'. It is the name used to describe a type and technique of singing which became fashionable in the 1600s, the Baroque period.

These days everyone is familiar with talent shows on the television where contestants sing to a panel and audience and are rated for their efforts. The early days of Bel Canto singing were much the same with singers and instrumentalists playing in concert halls to paying audiences. However, in the 1600s the musical shows were not amplified in any way and the audiences were noisy. To keep the attention of the audiences each show tried to outshine previous performances by increasing the visual presentation and showcasing the talent and virtuosity of the singers. Both instrumentalists and singers demonstrated their abilities in outdoing the other in playing and singing complex and rapid passages. The best singers, who could be heard over the orchestra and sung the most intricate passages, became the most popular and their teachers the most sought after.

The fashion for Bel Canto singing was suggested by Celletti (1991) to be driven by those composing opera: the composers and librettists. The instrumentalists and singers responded to the works offered and those with the most dexterity and ability were successful and their shows were popular. Celletti suggests that at that time the lower voices, baritone and tenor, were considered commonplace, whereas the higher voices were seen as lighter, more able to trill and add notes to a phrase. The manner in which the pool of soprano voices was maintained was quite shocking. The purity of the voice of young boys had always been valued in church singing: to maintain this high, treble sounding voice in adult singers, boys with promising voices, singing in the Sistine Chapel in Rome, were castrated so that their voice would not 'break'.

This produced men (castrati) with the vocal range of boys and women but with an adult's lung capacity. Those who went on to become opera singers were easily able to sing over a noisy audience.

Stark (1938) considers that the techniques of Bel Canto singing were established before the castrati became popular, but is in agreement that the castrati gained great popularity in the 1700s and early 1800s and that many earned more money than the opera composers themselves. Overall the castrati dominated Italian opera for 200 years and the methods used to train them became honed during that time.

Giambattista Mancini (1776) wrote about Carlo Broschi, known as Farinelli, one of the most famous operatic castrato singers with a voice that could range over three octaves. His singing teacher, Nicola Porpora, developed breathing exercises for him to develop the 'silent breath' and the agility needed to sing the fast, complex arias which were written for him by his brother Riccardo Broschi. Mancini noted that Farinelli's voice,

> was considered perfect, beautiful and sonorous in its quality and unparalleled in range ... The perfect art of holding the breath, and retaking it with such cleanness, so as to not allow anyone to know when he was breathing, started and ended with him. The perfect intonation, the unfolding, the extending and expanding of the voice ... the sparkling agility, and perfect trill were all in him in the same degree of perfection.

The Queen of Spain at that time thought Farinelli's voice might cure King Philip V's depression (Okutman, 2008).

There is a film about the brothers Farinelli – *Il Castrato* (1995) directed by Gérard Cobiau – which dramatizes their lives. Although not suitable for young viewers it does show the atmosphere of the opera houses and the rivalry between castrati in those days. It is noted that the voices of Farinelli, Caffarelli, and Senesino, castrati superstar singers, moved audiences to tears and standing ovations. Castrati were still singing in the 18–19th centuries, but by the late 19th and early 20th centuries the ethics of subjecting boys to castration brought this to an end (Jenkins, 2000). The last castrato, Alessandro Moreschi, was recorded at the end of his singing career in some of the earliest sound recordings. The purity and clear sound of his voice especially in the upper notes, with no or very little vibrato, can be heard clearly. This quality is just one of the characteristics of the Bel Canto sound.

The teaching methods used to train all singers at this time were closely guarded. Teachers were reluctant to give away any hints of their training and it was not written down. The one book that seems to have survived from that time is by Giambattista Mancini (1776). It has some surprisingly familiar themes about teachers and pupils of singing. From what can be gleaned from the literature, pupils would have practised humming for many years (Giles, 2006). Pupils would also have been encouraged to make the sound their teacher wanted for each vowel and then repeat it over and over again until all vowels could be reproduced accurately at all times.

Voice production and Bel Canto technique

At the turn of the 20th century the way in which the voice was produced was subjected to scientific investigation. The vocal folds (cords) are believed to have been first observed by Manuel Garcia II who is said to have invented the laryngoscope in the 1850s (Stark, 1938), and the vocal cords examined using stroboscopic illumination by Oertel in 1878 (Courey *et al.*, 2010). Garcia wrote extensively about singing technique and promoted the scientific study of voice production. His views were not widely prevalent at the time, the traditional teaching being based on the views of Francesco Lamperti (Stark, 1938).

Interest in Bel Canto as a method of training singers has continued in a small way since the early years and some textbooks with a modern interpretation and some new ideas have been written about this style of singing. Lucie Manén presented *The Art of Singing* in 1974 and a book on Bel Canto in 1977, which puts forwards some suggestions about how Bel Canto techniques work. Miller (1996) quite correctly notes that no modern teacher can honestly trace a historical lineage back to a particular Bel Canto teacher and that different and sometimes opposing techniques have become associated with the term throughout the years.

Bel Canto technique has not only been used by classical and operatic singers. Mario Lanza was a very well known and admired singer in the 1940s, who not only sang operatic arias but also Italian folk songs and popular songs in concerts and films. It was said that he trained laboriously with exercises until he could sing for hours without becoming tired, and had a voice that could project without any mechanical assistance in theatres as large as London's Royal Albert Hall (McGovern, 2011). He sang with two others in a group called the Bel Canto Trio, singing 86 concerts within one year. Frank Sinatra studied Bel Canto and used the General Italian pronunciation to produce open and clear diction (Morris, 2010). Tony Bennett and Dean Martin also studied Bel Canto; they became known as 'Crooners'.

An internet article on Tony Bennett notes,

> Forget cough drops. To preserve his voice after six decades of recording albums and performing, Bennett relies on a discipline called the Bel Canto method. He calls it 'the art of beautiful music' and says that 'by doing 15 or 20 minutes of Bel Canto, it gives you a center and places your voice correctly, so that when you sing, it appears quite effortless'. (Deutsch, 2011)

Modern Bel Canto

Today much is known and published about the structure and functions of the larynx and the vocal tract. The vibratory patterns of the vocal folds during singing can be followed over weeks and years in singers using laryngeal stroboscopy and evaluations made against standardized checklists to determine any problems (Courey *et* al., 2010). The differences in the way the entire vocal tract is used by Bel Canto trained singers compared to those singing in Musical Theatre has been studied and evaluated and it is generally agreed that well-trained classical singers have lower laryngeal muscle tension than the nonclassical (Koufman *et al.*, 1996).

We can recognize those singers using the Bel Canto technique by their posture, which appears at ease and relaxed, as if there is no effort or strain in singing; their breathing pattern, which flows freely and smoothly; and their voice which is clear with a 'silver bell-like' quality to the sound, and flows evenly and smoothly through all the notes and passages. The pronunciation of open Italian vowels and quick articulation of consonants are very clear and even on the quietest notes the voice will ring and travel through the auditorium. The overall sound will be full, resonant, and crystal-like.

Good vibrations

The production of sound is complex, but so also is the way in which the ears hear it and the brain perceives and interprets it. Some understanding of what sound is, how it is described, and some peculiarities of how we hear it as music is very relevant to the Bel Canto technique described in this book.

Objects have a natural frequency of vibration; if they are blown or tapped they will emit a sound if the blowing or tapping is continued. For example, if air is blown across the top of a bottle at a speed that matches the natural frequency of the bottle, an audible sound is produced. Similarly if you run a damp finger around the top of a wineglass at the correct speed, the glass will produce an audible tone. Some people play tunes on a succession of glasses filled with different amounts of liquid (this changes the volume of air in each glass). It is a useful concept to think of the glass producing such a sound as a happy glass. The energy put into the edge of the glass by running a finger around it makes the glass vibrate at exactly the right frequency and the glass effectively lets you know what that frequency is by resonating so you can hear the sound. Singing in some rooms, particularly bathrooms where the tiled surfaces bounce the sound back freely, produces the same effect and reveals the natural frequency or resonance of the room.

In Bel Canto singing a wonderful mixture of sound production occurs, involving air from the lungs vibrating the edge of the vocal folds in the larynx. The vibrating air is directed through the open tube of the pharynx and into the nasal cavities, where it passes across the openings of the complex shaped air sinuses in the facial bones. This can be thought of as similar to blowing across multiple little bottlenecks, resonating the air within them. When the passage of air is controlled and sustained all the air sinuses resonate at the same time. It can feel as if the sound is filling the head and being outside the body at the same time.

When instruments play the same tone at exactly the same frequency they produce harmonics, where more tones are heard than are being played. It is the production of harmonics that gives musical instruments their richness or timbre. When a group of Bel Canto singers sing together and match the production of their vowel sounds they also create harmonics and richness to the sound.

The setting in which singing occurs is intrinsically linked to the perception and interpretation of musical sound by the audience. Historically, the design of old churches and cathedrals promoted the resonance of the singing voice, so that sung call and response could be clearly heard at the back of the building over the congregation. Opera houses and concert halls were similarly built with the acoustics of the building in mind. Bel Canto singers, when singing in churches and older concert halls without the use of microphones or any amplification of the sound, are aware of the resonances occurring in their own body and know that the audience can feel as well as hear Bel Canto singing. Audience members often remark that the sound resonance causes their own head air sinuses to vibrate as well and they can feel the music in their body.

Chapter 2
Vocal anatomy and applying Bel Canto technique

This part of the book introduces the reader to the terms that describe the parts of the body used when singing (Figure 1). It has been arranged such that it follows the breath in and out of the body. After each part of the system has been described you will be asked to look in a mirror (a full length mirror is ideal) and then undertake a particular exercise. Many of the regions and structures used in singing cannot be seen easily and your imagination will also be needed to develop your own visual images to help you sing. A full singing warm up is given in Chapter 6.

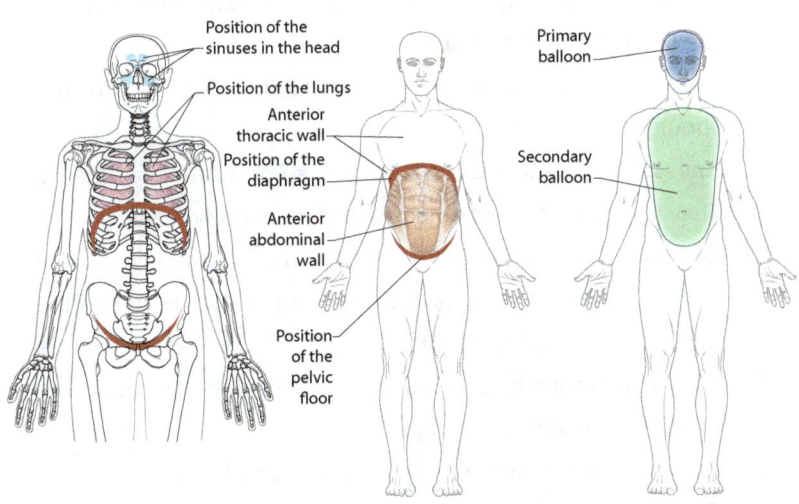

Figure 1: An overview of the main areas of the body used in singing. Observe the position of the pelvic floor, anterior abdominal wall, diaphragm, lungs, and air sinuses in the head. Note the idea of primary and secondary balloons to explain and for you to feel where inhaled air is.

Posture

When standing ready to sing your feet should be slightly apart making sure the knees are not locked, the back should be straight as if being stretched upwards and the coccyx tucked down. The head and chin face straight forward. The jaw must be relaxed, loose, and in its natural position, never pulled downwards, pushed forwards, or allowed to become stiff. The tongue is kept flat and forward with no tension allowing space for the air to flow without hindrance. The shoulders should always be relaxed and down and the thorax open to allow the ribs to swing out freely when the lungs are filled with air. The neck and shoulders are the areas that have a tendency to become tight, so we need to be very aware of relaxing them.

Observation 1: Posture

1. **Stand** in front of a mirror and look at your posture from toes to head. Are you standing upright?
2. **Feet** – Place the feet slightly apart lining them up with the shoulders.
3. **Knees** – Check the knees are not locked or pushed backwards. They must be loose but able to support the body securely.
4. **Coccyx** – Tuck the coccyx (lowest part of your spine) down. This helps prevent the back from being too curved and moves the pelvis into the correct position.
5. **Back** – Make sure the back is straight. Imagine that you are being pulled up toward the ceiling.
6. **Anterior abdominal wall** – This should be relaxed.
7. **Chest** (thorax) – Open the chest outwards. This will give a feeling of pushing the chest out. Be careful not to pull in or tighten the anterior abdominal wall as this is important for breathing.
8. **Shoulders** – Give the shoulders a little roll backwards to encourage them to open outwards and relax.

9. **Arms** – Let them hang loosely down by the side. The hands must also be relaxed.
10. **Head and Chin** – Make sure the head is facing straight forward without the chin being pushed forwards.
11. **Jaw** – Let the jaw hang in its natural relaxed position. It must not be clenched and the upper and lower teeth should not be touching.
12. **Tongue** – Let the tongue fall flat, forwards and relaxed in the bottom of the mouth. Feel the tip of the tongue lightly lean against the back of the lower front teeth.
13. **Cheeks and Smile** – Lift cheeks as a small smile keeping a relaxed jaw and tongue

---

Breathing

It is important to remember that breathing is automatic. When we are born, we all breathe as nature intended, as we do when crying to make a loud sound to attract attention. In young children the lungs expand naturally and the air is expelled naturally with no effort. A child vocalizing can be heard at great distances. Some of us, as adults, lose the ability to breathe naturally, so we must go back and think about this to be able to sing freely.

Breathing for singing

Sound is generated in the larynx when air passes between the vocal folds, so the control of breathing in and out, when and how you want to, is important for producing the singing voice. The muscles used to breathe in (inspiration) are the diaphragm, which extends across the trunk beneath the ribs, and the intercostal muscles between the ribs. When breathing in deeply the ribs move upwards and outwards, the diaphragm contracts moving downwards, and the abdominal wall moves out. All these movements draw air down the trachea and into the lungs. The lungs are surrounded by the ribs. They are positioned much higher than people think, with the base of the lungs level with the lowest point of the sternum at the front. The base of the lungs follows the contour of the diaphragm and extends lower at the sides and to a hands-breadth above the waist at the back.

When breathing in to sing, the air must fill all parts of the lungs, giving a feeling of an expanded chest and lower back (Figure 2). This is very important. Usually people do not fill their lungs fully when breathing in; they especially do not fill the lower parts of the lungs at the back.

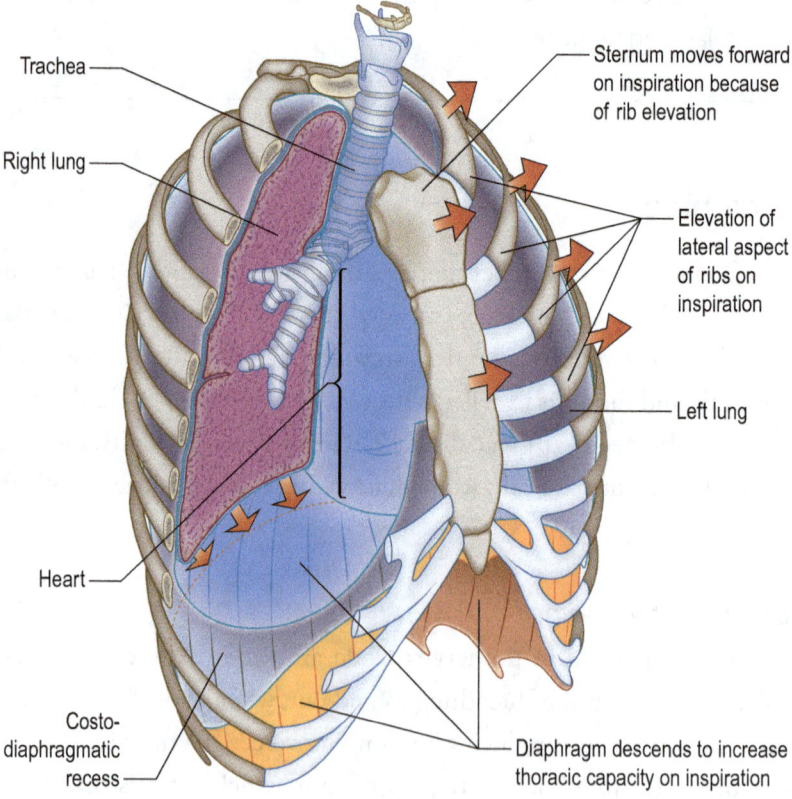

Figure 2: Diagram showing the expansion of the thorax when breathing in. The ribs swing outwards and upwards, the sternum moves forwards, the diaphragm moves downwards. When breathing in correctly the anterior abdominal wall moves outwards.

Normally when breathing out we just stop breathing in and let the elastic tissue in the lungs recoil and expel the air. In singing, control when breathing in and support when breathing out produces the correct air speed and pressure to produce sound. The legato (smooth and constant) breath flow carries the sound and creates resonance and harmonics throughout the vocal tract and resonating spaces. Breath support and constant air flow enable the singer to focus the sound. The lower anterior abdominal wall and pelvic floor muscles are very important in controlling breathing out, supporting and pushing the air from the lower parts of the lungs to replace what has been used in the upper parts, ensuring you can use all the air taken into the lungs.

Observation 2: Breathing

To appreciate the position of your body and the muscles used in breathing.

1. **Stand** in front of a mirror.
2. **Breathe** in through the nose taking in a full breath.
3. **Visualize** the inside of the nostrils flaring open at the same time as breathing in. Breathing in through the nose will warm and clean the air and encourage the sensation of the air passing through the nasal cavity and into the head sinuses as well as filling the lungs.
4. **Blow** the air out through the front of the lips and over the top teeth, as if blowing out a candle or blowing a feather away.
5. **Notice** what happens to the shoulders, chest, upper and lower abdomen, and ribs.
    Q. Do the shoulders go up when breathing in and down when breathing out or do they stay in the same relaxed position?
    A. They should remain in an open relaxed position at all times and never lift upward or push downward.

Q. Do the chest, abdomen, or ribs pull in or push down when breathing in or do they expand outwards?

A. They should expand outwards with the lower abdomen moving downwards when breathing in. The lower abdomen slowly moves inwards when blowing the air out.

Q. Are you aware of your abdominal wall and pelvic floor muscles?

A. These muscles reflexively tense up when you cough or laugh. They should also have increased activity when you are controlling your breath.

It is important not to allow the abdomen and chest to collapse as this will restrict the free flow of air and may cause tension in the base of the pharynx, root of the tongue, and top of the chest. In addition to this we can also 'lean' the air against the lower ribs and lower abdominal muscles just with the initial movement of air, before allowing the abdominal wall to move inwards when releasing the air. It is very important that this action feels free and not tight or constricted in any way. This also encourages the muscles in the pelvic floor to support the breath. There are many exercises that give us control of our breathing, but in this book we will use just a few of them.

Observation 3: Breathing

To appreciate the sensations of breath flow

1. **Breathe** in through the nose and blow the air out through the nose, visualizing blowing the air **upwards** through the top of the head. No vocal sound is needed when trying this. Focus on the feeling of the muscles inside the nose and throat.
2. **Breathe** in through the nose again, but this time when blowing the air out imagine blowing the air **downwards** and out through

the nose. Focus again on the feeling of the muscles inside the nose and throat.

Q. Can you feel a difference in the way the muscles move?

A. When blowing the air downwards it will feel as if the muscles are pulling downwards, but when blowing the air upwards the muscles will feel lifted, more open, and the air will feel free-flowing. This is the correct way the air should be released. Always visualize it moving up through the nose, through the top of the head and the forehead.

3. **Imagine** the body has two balloons (see Figure 1). Balloon 1 is the head and balloon 2 is the chest down to the lower abdomen. The head balloon is the 'Primary' air and the chest and lower abdomen the 'Secondary' air.

4. **Breathe** in through the nose and visualize filling the two balloons. Now blow the air upwards through the nose and head and visualize the primary air balloon (head) remaining full with the air from the secondary air balloon (lower abdomen), replacing the air used from balloon 1. (Think of it like squeezing the bottom of a toothpaste tube and keeping all the toothpaste in the top part. This will only be empty when all the toothpaste has gone.)

5. Do this several times to become familiar with the sensation, making sure the back of the tongue does not lift up, tighten, or push against the roof of the mouth (hard palate).

Breathing exercises

When practising breathing exercises, and learning new songs, take a breath when you need to. Any extra breaths can be removed later when the muscles gain more control over air flow and the lungs are able to take in bigger and deeper breaths. It is much better to take a breath and not let the throat or chest squeeze when there is not enough air to sing through a phrase. If you constantly squeeze muscles due to lack of air this will become a habit and the muscles will become conditioned to doing this. Free flowing air creates a legato sound.

1. Filling the lungs

Take a full breath in through the nose, filling down to the bottom of the lungs, allowing the lower back, abdomen, and chest to expand. Blow all the air out quickly through the lips, focusing on blowing the air (without vocalizing) from the front of the lips and over the top teeth. WHOOOOOOOO. *Repeat this twice more.*

2. Sustained, smooth breath

Breathe in through the nose, filling right to the bottom of the lungs as described above, and release the air using a sissing sound. Do this by placing the tip of the tongue just behind the front teeth and keeping the lips open. Release the air at an even speed until all the air has gone by gently pulling in the pelvic floor. Keep the air flowing smoothly (the term for this is legato), never jerkily. *Repeat this exercise three times.*

The length of time it takes for the breath to be released may be quite short to begin with, but with practise it will become easier to sustain it for much longer. Try counting in seconds to see how long the air is able to flow out. Twenty seconds is good to begin with, although you may find that only ten or fifteen seconds are managed the first few times. With practise it will become possible to go for about forty-five seconds and maybe even more in time.

Each time a breath is taken in, try taking in a little more air than before to encourage the lungs, back, abdomen, and ribs to expand more with each breath. When breathing in, make sure that the abdomen is relaxed and the shoulders do not lift up. Over time, this will develop a smooth, steady, and supported air flow.

Production of the voice

Sound is produced in the larynx by expelled air vibrating the vocal folds. When a breath has been taken in and is expelled in the controlled way used in singing, the sound is modified as it passes upwards into the larynx and pharynx, where it is affected by the position of the tongue, the jaw, the shape of the mouth and lips, and the position of the uvula and soft palate. Each of these structures will be considered in turn.

Larynx and vocal folds

The larynx can be seen in the neck, where it is often termed the 'Adam's apple'. It is made of cartilage and ligaments and sits above the trachea, which conducts air to and from the lungs (Figure 3). Standing in front of a mirror you will be able to see where the two halves of the thyroid cartilage join at the front of your neck (laryngeal prominence). Watch this move up and down when you swallow. Above the larynx there is an angle where the vertical part of the neck changes to horizontal and the skin comes forward to the point of the chin: at this angle is the hyoid bone. Below the thyroid cartilage is a complete cartilage ring, the cricoid cartilage, on which sit two arytenoid cartilages, which provide the origin of the vocal folds (cords) and permit them to move.

Intrinsic laryngeal muscles attach to the laryngeal cartilages to move them. The whole structure is covered with a mucous membrane which- that forms part of the vocal apparatus. Viewed from the back the mucous membrane stretches from each side of the epiglottis to right and left arytenoid cartilages (Figure 4). As this passes downwards it forms the false vocal folds (cords) and then the vocal folds (cords) on

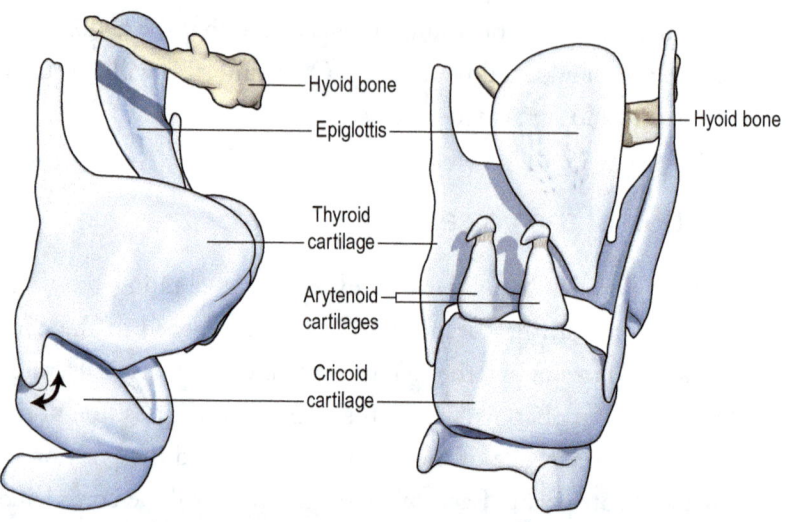

Figure 3: The larynx from the right side (left) and from the back (right).

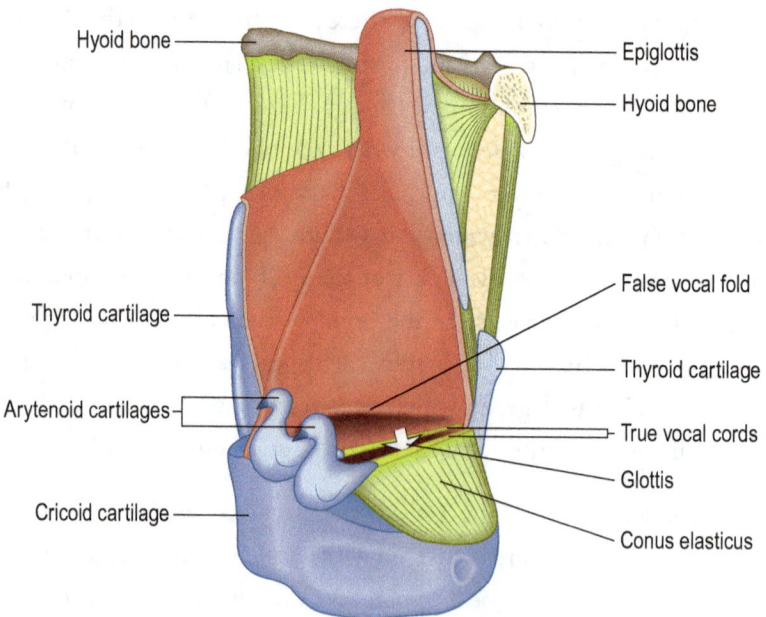

Figure 4: The larynx from the back showing the vocal folds (cords) attached to the arytenoid cartilages. The vocal cords are made of the free edge of the conus elasticus, supported by a thin muscle, vocalis.

CHAPTER 2: VOCAL ANATOMY AND APPLYING BEL CANTO TECHNIQUE

each side, before continuing inside the cricoid cartilage and into the trachea. The vocal folds are supported internally by an elastic membrane (conus elasticus) and a very small muscle (vocalis). The space between the vocal folds where the air passes, the glottis, is controlled by movements of the arytenoid cartilages.

When puffs of air pass up through the larynx the tissues of the vocal folds (cords) vibrate (Figure 5). When singing the vocal cords are

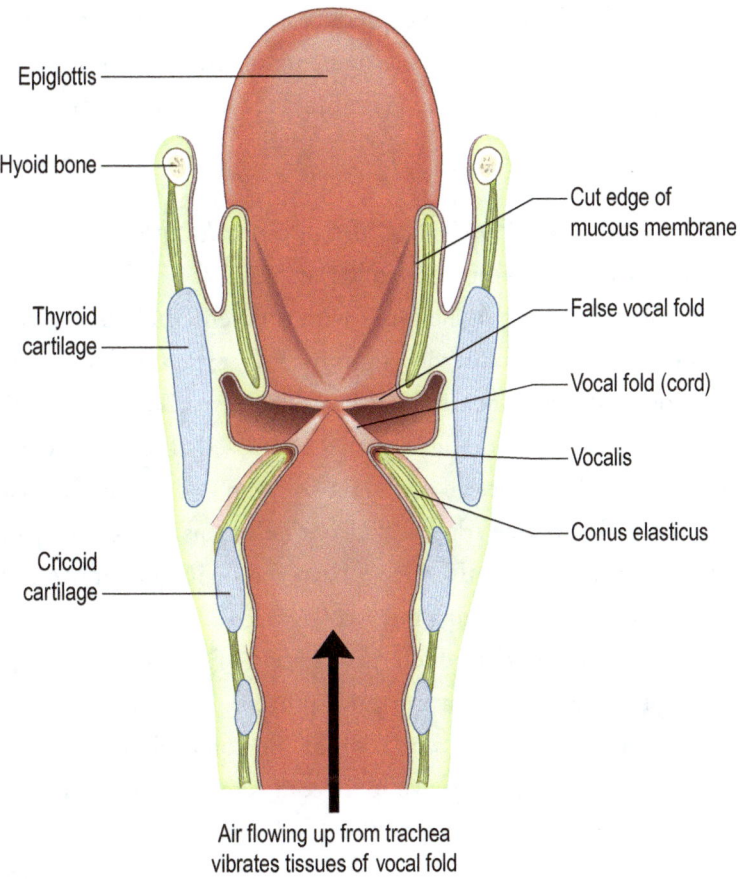

Figure 5: Coronal section through the larynx. The vocal folds (cords) are structures made of the mucous membrane covering the free edge of the conus elasticus and vocalis muscle. Air passing upwards from the trachea produces vibrations of these tissues when the vocal folds are brought together by the cricoarytenoid muscles.

tensed and held close together by surrounding muscles and a sustained breath is pushed out. This is the basis of singing vowel sounds. The pitch of the note is changed by changes in the length of the vocal cords. The loudness is changed by the force of air puffed between the vocal cords. The quality of the sound, or timbre, describes whether the sound is harsh or mellow and pleasing to the ear. It is affected by the edges of the vocal folds (cords) and how they vibrate. If the vocal folds (cords) become thickened or swollen, for example when you have a cough and cold, then the sound produced if you try to sing is hoarse and harsh. Experienced singers aim at singing on the 'rim of the fold (cord)', a part of the edge of the vocal folds (cords), which produces a very clear, edgy sound.

Details of vocal fold (cord) structure and production of sound

The terms vocal cords or vocal folds are used for structures which contain many different tissue types with different abilities to stretch, contract, and respond to the vibrations made by expiratory air. On each side the deepest structure, the conus elasticus (also called the cricothyroid ligament or cricovocal ligament), is composed of connective tissue (fibrocytes which synthesize abundant collagen and elastin fibres and other proteins). The free edge of the conus elasticus is also termed the vocal ligament; it is slightly thicker than the main part of the conus elasticus, meaning it contains more collagen and elastin. It is covered by a small muscle, vocalis, which runs from the front of the inner part of the thyroid cartilage to a muscular process on the arytenoid cartilage. Vocalis tenses as the free edge of the conus elasticus vibrates. Over both structures is a layer of loose connective tissue, composed of fibrocytes, which make collagen fibres, and a water-holding jelly-like protein which holds the collagen fibres apart. The final layer, facing the inside of the larynx, is termed a mucous membrane; it is similar to the skin inside the mouth and pharynx. It is composed of two types of tissue, a stratified squamous epithelium, specialized for wear and tear, and an underlying connective tissue layer, termed lamina propria

CHAPTER 2: VOCAL ANATOMY AND APPLYING BEL CANTO TECHNIQUE

(also composed of fibrocytes, collagen fibres, and water-holding jelly-like protein), which supports capillaries and nerves. The mucous membrane especially, along with the lower loose connective tissue layer, vibrates as air passes over each vocal cord.

When singing a pure vowel the vocal cords are closely apposed but do not quite touch (Figure 6). They are moved together by the lateral cricoarytenoid muscle on each side, plus transverse and oblique arytenoids muscles, and moved apart by the posterior cricoarytenoid muscle on each side. It is likely that when a singer feels they are singing on the 'rim of the cord', they have the ideal gap between the vocal cords, at the ideal tension and they generate the ideal vibration pattern.

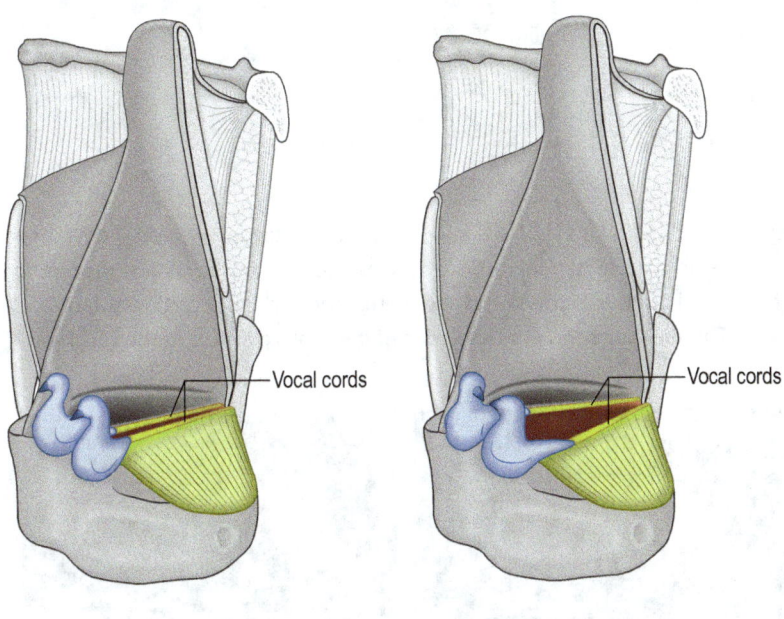

When the arytenoid cartilages are close together and in line on the cricoid cartilage the vocal cords are close together

When the arytenoid cartilages are apart and swivelled on the cricoid cartilage the vocal cords are apart

Figure 6: The vocal cords are moved together and apart by the actions of cricoarytenoid muscles. When singing, the vocal cords are held close but not touching.

When looking at the vocal cords in a person an endoscopic tube is used. Viewed this way the thyroid cartilage is at the front and the arytenoids cartilages at the back. The same movements as in Figure 6 are seen in Figure 7, but from the top (see also Figure 8).

When shouting and coughing the vocal cords move towards each other very rapidly and touch with quite a force, similar to smacking two bits of skin together. This can lead to the epithelium growing thicker along

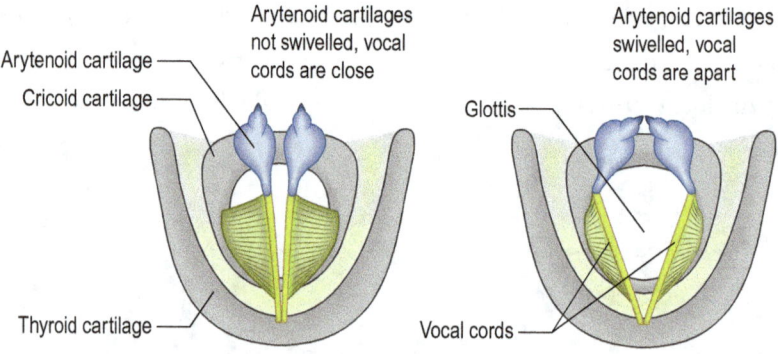

Figure 7: The thyroid, cricoid, and arytenoid cartilages viewed from above. Movements of the arytenoid cartilages on the cricoid cartilage change the position of the vocal cords and the size of the glottis. The arytenoid cartilages face backwards. This diagram shows the free edge of the conus elasticus as the vocal cord.

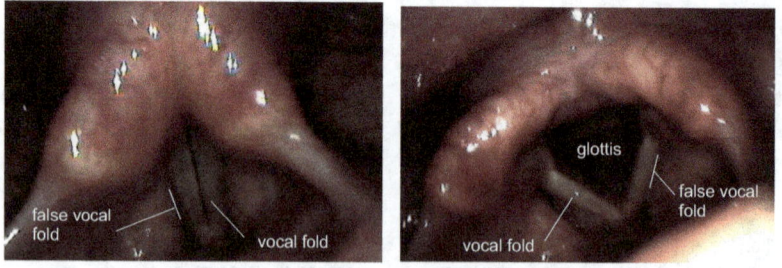

Figure 8: Note the closed glottis when singing and the open glottis when not singing. These photographs show the vocal folds, i.e. the vocal cords covered in a mucous membrane. (WIth permission of Mr. Declan Costello, consultant laryngologist.)

parts of the vocal cords, similar to calluses developing on the palms of the hands or soles of the feet because of increased friction. If the cords are more seriously damaged in this way (as if a blister forms and bursts on the feet) then a similar healing process occurs which also thickens the vocal cords. Such thickenings are called nodules. (They occur more frequently in children and females, those using their voice excessively, and in bad vocal technique (Altman, 2007)).

Pharynx and tongue

The neck is composed of vertebrae at the back and the structure termed the throat at the front. The 'throat' is a region where food is directed into the oesophagus at the back and air is directed into the trachea at the front. The part where both air and food pass is termed the pharynx. The pharynx extends from the back of the nasal cavities to the back of the larynx (Figure 9). You can often feel cold air touching the walls

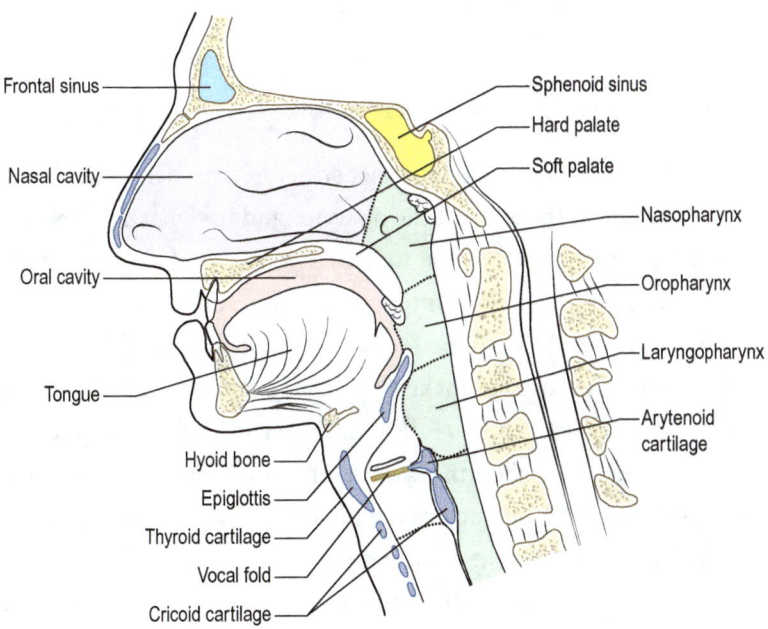

Figure 9: The parts of the pharynx, mouth, and nasal cavity used in singing. Note the hard and soft palate, epiglottis, and position of the vocal folds.

of the pharynx when you breathe in on a cold day, and you can feel hot drinks in the pharynx as they pass down from the mouth into the oesophagus.

If you look at the inside of your mouth in the mirror you can see some of the structures in the oral cavity and the wall of the oropharynx (Figure 10).

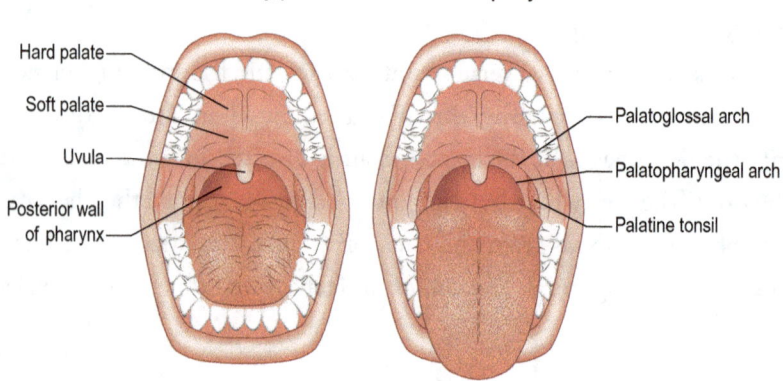

Figure 10: Oral and pharyngeal structures that can be seen in the mouth.

The tongue is a highly mobile muscular structure attached to the hyoid bone, the lower jaw, the walls of the pharynx, and to the palate. You can only see about two-thirds of the tongue if you look at your mouth in the mirror, even if you stick your tongue out. The very back third of the tongue is vertical and cannot be seen (Figure 9). The tip of the tongue is very mobile and is used to make consonant sounds, try the following sounds '–l-', '-t-', '-d-', and '-s-'. The back portion of the tongue you can see is sometimes called the 'saddle' of the tongue in singing. The vertical portion of the tongue has a tendency to lift up and backwards when singing, restricting the flow and resonance of air in the pharynx. To prevent this, the tongue should be kept flat in the mouth and the back of the tongue kept forwards at all times. The tip of the tongue can be placed behind the lower front teeth to help achieve this.

Observation 4: Inside the mouth

To examine tongue movements

1. Stand in front of a mirror and look at your tongue, note you are only seeing about 2/3rds of it. Put your tongue out and draw it backwards and forwards a few times, flattening it so you can feel its sides touching the back teeth.
2. Watch your tongue as you make the 'l', 't', 'd', and 's' sounds by flicking the tip of your tongue against your upper teeth
3. Next look at the back of your tongue and make the sounds NGAA, GAA, and YAA. Only move the back of the tongue for the NGAA and GAA and only the sides for the YAA, making sure the front of the tongue does not rise up in the mouth and remains completely forward. This is very important. When making the YAA sound notice that the tongue will move backwards and forwards very slightly in the mouth with the tip of the tongue staying against the back of the front bottom teeth.

Mental visualization of tongue movements

4. Firstly, with closed lips, relax the jaw making sure not to push it forwards or downwards.
5. Visualize the tongue lying flat on the floor of the mouth making sure it does not touch the roof of the mouth and is not moving. Visualize it slowly moving forward and feel it pushing against the bottom teeth.
6. Visualize the back, 'saddle', of the tongue, also moving forward and staying flat in the mouth

You are not physically performing these last exercises, only thinking them through using visualization and your imagination. To begin with, there may not be any sensation of tongue movement, but with continued practise, the tongue will gradually start to move on its own.

Mouth, palate, uvula, and fauces

Compare Figure 10 to the view of the inside of your own mouth as you look in the mirror. The tongue forms the floor of the mouth. The roof of the mouth is formed by the palate. Place the tip of your tongue behind the front top teeth and take it backwards over the roof of the mouth. This is the hard palate. Now move it further back until you feel a change from hard to soft. This is now the soft palate. Do not go any further back as it may cause a gagging sensation.

The hard palate separates the mouth from the nasal cavities; it is made of bone. The soft palate is a mobile flap containing muscle, which is attached to the back of the hard palate. It hangs down vertically between the mouth and pharynx with a midline process called the uvula (Figure 11). The uvula has no function in singing except that it

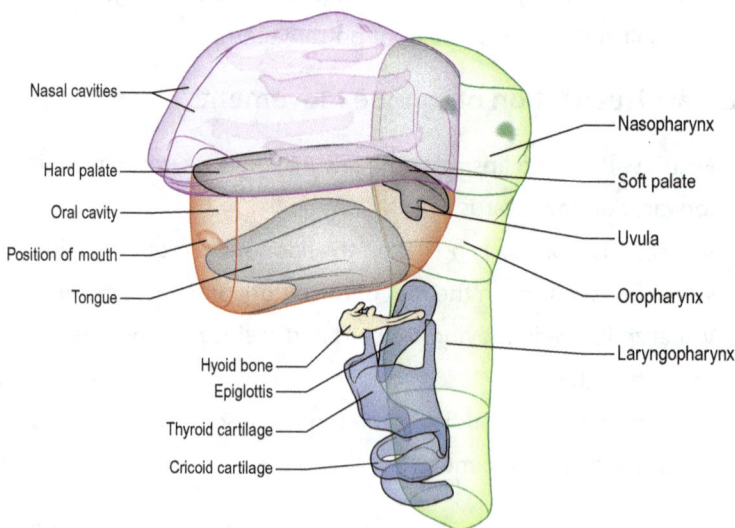

Figure 11: This shows a diagrammatic representation of a 3D view of the mouth, nasal cavity, and pharynx. You can see the hard palate, soft palate, and uvula at the back of the oral cavity. Being able to visualize and imagine your palate is very important in Bel Canto singing.

CHAPTER 2: VOCAL ANATOMY AND APPLYING BEL CANTO TECHNIQUE

must be raised. To produce a resonant sound, the muscles in the soft palate are encouraged to contract and lift and stretch sideways. It is very important that this lift and stretch is maintained on all notes at all times and is mentally increased on descending notes to help create a fuller resonant and open sound. It is natural for this lift to occur when singing higher tones but not when singing lower ones.

If you look in the mirror at your soft palate and uvula you will be able to see it lift if you say 'aaah'. Beyond the soft palate is the pharynx wall. You will also see that the curve of the soft palate blends with the sides of the mouth and the tongue. You may be able to see your tonsils if you still have them. The folds in front and behind the tonsils are called the fauces (pronounced forseees). They contain muscles that attach the soft palate to the wall of the pharynx (behind) and to the tongue (in front).

When singing, the fauces need to be stretched outwards (as wide as possible) to create the open vowels and part of the open pharynx (Figure 12). To help create the lift at the back and sides of the pharynx,

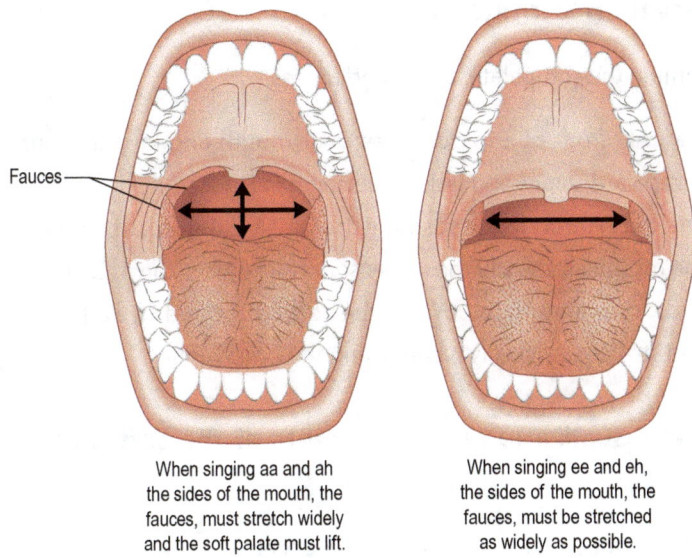

When singing aa and ah the sides of the mouth, the fauces, must stretch widely and the soft palate must lift.

When singing ee and eh, the sides of the mouth, the fauces, must be stretched as widely as possible.

Figure 12: Note the different shape of the fauces and the lift of the palate when singing different vowels.

a small smile is needed which lifts the upper lip and cheek muscles without tightening the jaw.

Try lifting the cheeks in a small smile and then relaxing the smile a few times to feel the muscles lifting at the back of the pharynx. Do not pull the sides of the lips out too much as this can then become too tight. It is possible to lift the soft palate without the use of the smile, but you will notice that the fauces do not move outwards as easily. The beginning of the yawn mechanism also causes these stretching movements of the fauces and soft palate and is helpful to feel the position needed when singing. The second part of the yawn, which pulls the tongue downwards, must not be used.

The joint between the upper and lower jaws can be felt when you place your fingers just in front of your ears. When singing, the lower jaw should feel relaxed and the mouth opened just enough to fit a fingertip between your teeth.

Observation 5: Inside the mouth

To examine the soft palate, uvula, and fauces.

1. Stand in front of a mirror, open your mouth and identify your soft palate, uvula, and fauces as shown in Figure 10.
2. Breathe in through the nose and then release the breath through the mouth as you say the vowel sound AAAAH on an ascending and descending pitch. Watch the soft palate and uvula lift up and stretch, especially when taking the pitch higher.

Mental visualization of movements of the soft palate and fauces

Do not rush this. It takes time and persistence!

3. With your eyes closed, visualize the uvula lifting upwards, the soft palate widening and lifting up towards the top of the head. Focus on this until the muscles can be felt lifting and stretching.
4. Now visualize the fauces moving outwards. They are not something you might have imagined before so may take longer to control. They may stretch outwards only a little to begin with and then spring back. This is normal but, with practise, they will eventually stretch outwards and stay in this position.
5. Try visualizing all this together. Do not physically do this exercise, use visualization and mental control only!

Repeat this as many times as you like to encourage muscle memory.

Many singing teachers refer to the 'open throat' when describing the pharynx. This includes the following actions:

- The soft palate and uvula are lifted.
- The fauces are stretched sideways.
- The whole of the tongue is flat and forward in the mouth.
- The tip of the tongue against the back of the lower front teeth.
- The naso, oro and laryngopharynx are as open and unobstructed as possible.

Imposto and the nasal air sinuses, resonance and humming

Air from the lungs passes between the vocal cords into the pharynx and is normally directed over the soft and hard palates and through the nasal cavities. The two nasal cavities are separated by a midline bony septum. The air comes out of the external nose, which is made of cartilage with a cartilage septum. The sides of the nasal cavities communicate with air sinuses in the frontal, sphenoid, ethmoid, and maxillary bones.

There are three pairs of sinuses and one midline sinus (Figure 13). The largest are the maxillary sinuses between the eyes (above) and upper teeth (below) on each side; these can become infected in cases of sinusitis. The ethmoidal sinuses are between the eyes and the midline on each side; they are arranged as many small communicating spaces. The frontal sinuses are above each eye; often you can feel the cold air in them when walking out on a very cold day. The single sphenoidal sinus is behind the level of the eyes in the midline.

When directing the air upwards and through the nasal cavities the air flow passes across the openings of the air sinuses and they resonate, like blowing across the top of a bottle. When this happens the head feels full of sound. The ears also have a connection on each side to the nasal cavities and sometimes the resonance can also be felt in them (Figure 14).

Achieving this resonance of the air sinuses in the head is called 'placing' or, to give it its correct Italian term, 'imposto' (Figure 15). It is the connection of the flowing air from the larynx, through the pharynx, through the soft palate and connecting with the frontal, ethmoidal, and maxillary sinuses.

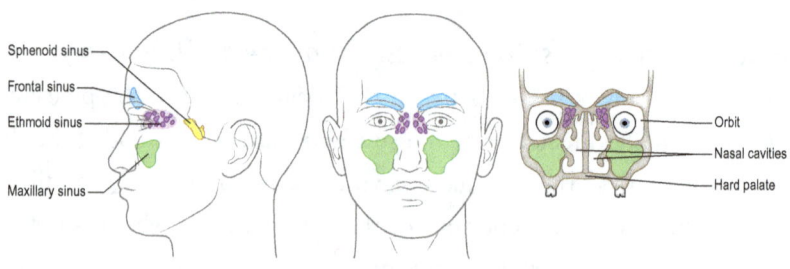

Figure 13: Showing the air sinuses in the head. The internal structure of the nasal cavity is shown on the right. All of the sinuses are lined with the same epithelium as the nasal cavity.

CHAPTER 2: VOCAL ANATOMY AND APPLYING BEL CANTO TECHNIQUE

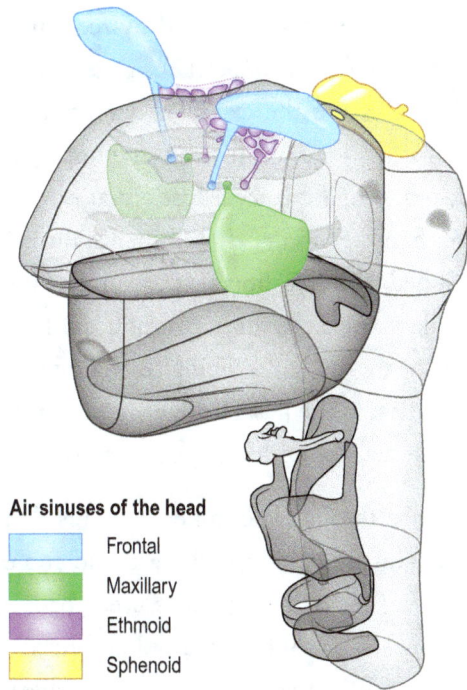

Air sinuses of the head
- Frontal
- Maxillary
- Ethmoid
- Sphenoid

Figure 14: When singing, the air passes through the pharynx, over the hard palate, into the nasal cavities and across the openings of the air sinuses. . The air sinuses of the head resonate when the speed and direction of the air flow is just right.

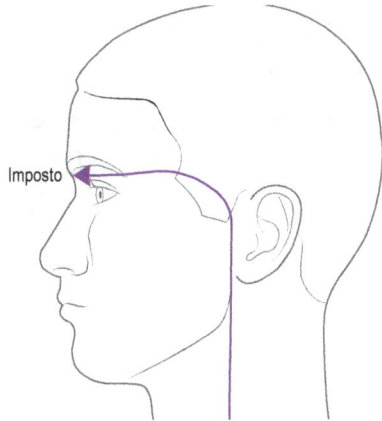

Figure 15: Showing the direction of air to the imposto.

The resonation of the imposto has been demonstrated by recording vibration during use of resonant voice (Yiu *et al.*, 2012). A piezoelectrical accelerometer was used to measure the extent of vibration at the laryngeal prominence and at the bridge of the nose (the imposto) during use of normal, strained, and resonant voice. More vibration was noted at the bridge of the nose than the laryngeal prominence during resonant voice. The study concluded that vibration at the bridge of the nose reflected the extent of resonant voice the subjects produced. They noted that this finding supports the method of teaching resonant voice which relies on the physical sensation at the nasal bridge and that resonant voice phonation reduced the tension of the laryngeal muscles.

Thus the development of resonance through the imposto means that those trained in Bel Canto technique can sing with ease and more effectively for a much longer time. The resonating areas used for Bel Canto technique are: all head bones and frontal, ethmoid and maxillary sinuses. Vibration can also be felt in the palate, top teeth, cheek bones (maxillae), and at the back of the head.

Recognizing the sensations of the imposto

When the air is connected and flowing through the imposto the singer may experience various sensations:

- Vibrations in the forehead.
- Eyes may feel as though they are vibrating.
- Tingling in the top and back of the head.
- If the sound is very powerful and on a high note it can cause the skull to feel as if it is swaying from side to side with a feeling of dizziness.
- The sound is edgy and powerful.
- Much easier than you would expect to produce the singing sound.
- More control over dynamics.

Once the use of the imposto is mastered the dynamic interpretation of a song, i.e. the ability to sing a note getting louder and then softer on one breath (*messa di voce*) becomes much easier to control.

The sigh

Breathe in through the nose and feel the air in the pharynx, around the soft palate and uvula. Release this air as if sighing, taking it over the soft palate. Now breathe in again and release the air as if sighing on the vowel sound AAH. Feel the air as it flows across the soft palate. Note that your pelvic floor and lower abdominal muscles must be supporting the sigh.

Humming Exercises

Breathe in through the nose making sure the tongue is flat and forward in the mouth, keeping it completely away from the roof of the mouth, and mentally visualize the air filling the primary air balloon (the head). It will of course fill the secondary air balloon (chest to lower abdomen) as well, even though we are focusing on the primary air balloon to begin with.

Hum with lips closed and the tip of the tongue behind the top teeth as for 'n'.

1. Make one long continuous hum HNNNNNN through the bridge of the nose by blowing the air upwards and forwards, sending it through the forehead.
2. Make shorter consecutive hums by re-articulating the blowing of the air in the same position as the long HNNNNNN.

Humming is similar to *whimpering*. Think of a puppy whimpering and the sound it makes. This action takes the air up through the nasal cavities and maxillary and connects with the ethmoidal and frontal sinuses.

Feel the pressure behind the nose and eyes and the vibration in the forehead, top teeth and upper lip. There should also be a buzzing sensation. Do this again and think of whimpering, at the same time making sure the throat does not become involved. The whimper is also sometimes called the 'operatic sob'.

> Q. Does this feel as though the air is high and focused in the head and can you feel a 'tapping' sensation in the forehead?
> A. If it does, then this is correct.

Focusing the hum HNN through the individual nostrils and the *glissando*.

1. **Take** in a full breath through the nose, close one nostril by placing a finger against one side of the nose to close it, and hum HNN a scale downwards starting on the C above middle C. Re-articulate the air as described above, with the sound through the open nostril on each note, making sure the air never stops flowing.
2. **Change** nostrils and do the same through the other nostril. Note that one sinus is usually more blocked and so needs to be worked more with the HNN to clear it.
3. **Move** up the scale in semitones and repeat as high as feels comfortable.
4. **Now** start again from the C above middle C and HNN as described above, through both nostrils together. The air should feel high and forward in the head with vibrations being felt in the head and facial bone structure. If the throat feels tight, stop and check where the tongue is as it may be against the roof of the mouth. The lips can be closed or open. If open, make sure the tip of the tongue only is leaning against the back of the top front teeth to stop the air escaping through the mouth.
5. Now using both nostrils start on middle C and HNN up and down the octave in a glissando. Go up in semitones and do the same

exercise. Again, take this as high and as low as feels comfortable and HNN an octave at a time.

This, along with the breathing exercises, should be practised on a daily basis before starting any singing. It encourages the sinuses to become vibrant and flexible.

Chapter 3
Singing sounds

Production of vowels

Vowels are the parts of words that carry the breath when singing. Bel Canto singing technique was developed in Italy in the 17th century and uses the pure, open, and clear vowel sounds termed here the Italian vowels.

When talking about speech five vowel sounds are considered; however, spoken English includes many local dialects with the pronunciation of these vowel sounds varying in different parts of the country. Some written vowels are pronounced as if they change from one vowel sound to another when spoken. Thus although the word *bit* clearly has only one vowel sound *i*, the word *bite* has two joined vowel sounds, which could be *eye* and *ee* before the *t*, or perhaps *a* and *ee*, or even *uy* and *ii* before the *t*, depending on where you come from. In these cases, where two vowels are sounded on one syllable, it is called a diphthong. Often, when singing in English, the ending vowel sound of a diphthong pulls the fauces inwards and downwards and produces a dull and closed sound which makes the voice sound old and dark. The sung Italian language uses pure vowel sounds without diphthongs. Singing these vowels keeps the soft palate lifted, the fauces stretched widely, and the pharynx open, producing a pure, open sound with a natural lightness, that keeps the voice sounding young and bright.

Twenty different vowel sounds have been identified in spoken language and each is represented by a specific symbol in the International Phonetic Alphabet. Words are often spelt out in phonetics in dictionaries to show readers how to pronounce them. The specific vowel sounds used in the singing exercises in this book are shown in the table as Italian vowels. They have been supplemented for singing songs in

English as well as Italian; the *i* sound as in *thin* is part of English pronunciation rather then Italian, and the vowel A in both languages can be sung with the fauces and tongue very widely stretched as in AA, or with the tongue even flatter and a feeling of greater vertical space in the pharynx as in AH. The phonetic sounds and example pronunciations of the vowels used in the exercises are given in Table 1. It is worth looking up these phonetic sounds on the internet to hear the sound of the vowel exactly: at the time of writing we can recommend the websites www.multimedia-english.com/phonetics/british-vowels and www.yorku.ca/earmstra/ipa/vowels.html.

English vowel	Italian vowel	Phonetic sound	Sound in word underlined
A	AA	æ	b<u>a</u>t
	AH	ɑː	<u>a</u>rm
E	EH	e	m<u>e</u>t
		ɪ	th<u>i</u>n
I	EE	iː	s<u>ee</u>
O	OH	ɒ	h<u>o</u>t
U	OO	uː	f<u>oo</u>d

Table 1: English and Italian vowels and their phonetic sounds.

Visualization

Begin with visualization of the soft palate, uvula, and fauces. Visualize the vowel AA, lifting the soft palate and pushing the fauces outwards, with tongue flat and forwards in the mouth. When singing vowels, mentally stretch your fauces outwards to keep the vowel pure and the pharynx open.

Vowel exercise

AA, EH, EE, OH, OO

1. Take a deep breath in, taking the air and the vowel to the soft palate. Sound out AA on one tone (normal speech level) as a supported breath exhalation, feel the air passing over the soft palate. Repeat this for each of the vowel sounds: EH, EE, OH, OO. The OO sound passes over the soft and hard palate and you can feel it in your top teeth and upper lip. You might be able to feel your lips and teeth vibrating. You must keep the breath supported and moving fast. The sound may be louder than you expect, but make sure you do not force the sound.

2. Take a deep breath in, move the air to the soft palate. Sound out AA moving the tone from a low tone to a higher tone and back down again. As the sound goes higher you may be able to feel it in your nasal cavity. Repeat this for each of the vowel sounds: EH, EE, OH, OO. The EE sound is very likely to be felt over your top teeth. As the tone becomes higher it may be felt in your head (Figure 16).

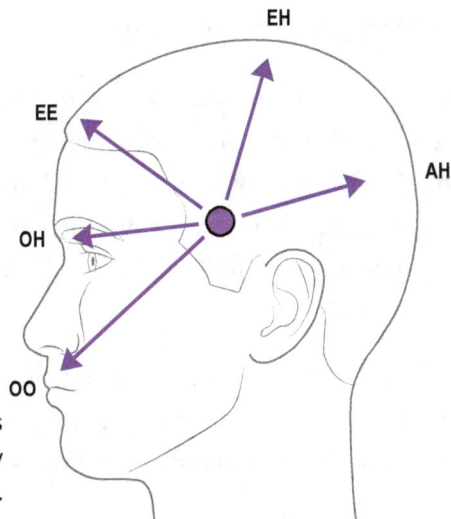

Figure 16: Resonant areas where the placed vowels may be felt, depending on the pitch..

Singing vowels

To achieve pure Italian vowel sounds when you sing needs a bit more thought than you might expect. When sung vowel sounds travel through the air to the ears of the listeners, its clarity may not be received as intended and the listener may not recognize the words. Because of this, when singing in Bel Canto technique, the vowel sound is adjusted at the outset, so if you read the lyrics of a song in Bel Canto in spoken voice they may sound rather strange, yet when they are sung the listener perceives the correct pronunciation. It is always worth saying a song aloud, using the Italian vowels, while smiling, lifting the soft palate, and stretching the fauces in preparation for singing. Remember, no Italian vowel has two sounds (a diphthong) within one vowel.

To ensure the words sung are always clear to the audience, the pronunciation of the Italian vowels is adjusted from the C above middle C and higher. At these pitches it is much harder to produce the OH and OO vowels clearly and the EE vowel can become squeaky. Therefore the AA and AH vowels are used for the very highest notes so the sound produced is clear and pure. The audience will still hear the words sung, even if the sung vowel is different on these top notes.

Production of consonants

Although the aim of singing is to maintain the vowel sounds for as long as possible, the clear articulation of consonants, especially at the beginning and end of words, is very important. Without their clear and quick articulation we would not understand the words. If too much time is spent on them the vowel will be shortened, also making the word unclear.

Each consonant must be clear but articulated quickly when singing so as not to take any sound away from the vowel. The first consonant of a word must be clear and distinct. Words starting with 'm', 'n', and 'l',

Lip	Sides of the tongue
M [B, P, W]	Y [J]
Tip of tongue	**Back of tongue and soft palate**
L, N [D, R, S, T, Z]	G [C, K, Q]
Lip and teeth	**Back of tongue, soft palate, and imposto**
V [F]	NG
Breath consonant	
H	

Table 2: Consonants and where they are formed.

help to get the air into the imposto, as does 'v' which is used on the breath focused in the bridge of the nose; they can be used as described in the warm up exercises. The consonants 't', 'd', and 'b' are approached differently at the beginning of a word than at the end. It is useful to begin with a short hum when articulating 'd' and 'b' at the beginning of a word.

The consonants at the end of words are invariably carried on to the beginning of the next word, so the vowel sound is clear for the duration of the note. Ending consonants followed by a breath use a different technique. Those such as 't' and 'd' are very important and can be sounded rapidly and clearly with a flick of the tip of the tongue behind the front, upper teeth. Consonants like 'ch' and 'g' (give), and 'j' (just, large) are formed further forward in the mouth than in speech. Ending on 'm' or 'n' needs a stress on the sound without stopping the breath.

Exercises to help you feel the vowels and consonants

MAH, MEH, MEE, MOH, MOO

The lip consonant M is helpful to find the placing at the imposto. Begin with a m (hm) against lightly closed lips and add it to the vowel. Sound the vowel in speech tone three times. Take a deep breath making sure the air fills the imposto.

Sing a descending scale from the C above middle C, using the sounds MEE – MAH on each note. Feel the muscles around the pharynx and fauces stretching higher and wider each time the vowel is sounded. Repeat this exercise moving up one semitone, as far as it feels comfortable, and down one semitone, as far as it feels comfortable.

To utilize all the vowels, take a deep breath making sure the air fills the imposto and sing a descending scale from the C above middle C, sounding MAH, MEH, MEE, MOH, MOO on each note. Again, repeat this exercise moving up one semitone, as far as it feels comfortable, and down one semitone, as far as it feels comfortable. The transition from one sound to the next is rapid, ensuring the air and vowels constantly flow through the imposto.

Tip of the tongue consonants

Take a deep breath making sure the air fills the imposto, put the tip of the tongue against the back of the top teeth and primary palate, hum the air through the bridge of the nose. This will encourage the resonance in the imposto.

Take another deep breath in, move the air to the soft palate. Sound out NNN, moving the tone from a low tone to a higher tone and back down again.

You should be able to feel this in your nasal cavity throughout. Whereas the M sound allows the air to come more forward into the mouth as well as the other resonant areas, the N sound takes the air higher and into the nasal cavity and frontal sinuses.

LAA, LEH, LEE, LOH, LOO

The N sound is helpful for finding the next tip of the tongue consonant, the L sound. Begin with a *n* sound, tongue against the back of the top teeth and primary palate, take a deep breath making sure the air fills the imposto, sing a descending scale from the C above middle C, using the sounds LEE – LAA on each note. Concentrate on the flexibility of the tip of the tongue and the resonance in the imposto. Ensure the pharynx and fauces are stretched higher and wider each time the vowel is sounded. Repeat this exercise moving up one semitone, as far as it feels comfortable and down one semitone, as far as it feels comfortable.

To utilize all the vowels, take a deep breath making sure the air fills the imposto and sing a descending scale from the C above middle C, sounding LAA, LEH, LEE, LOH, LOO on each note. Again repeat this exercise moving up one semitone, as far as it feels comfortable, and down one semitone, as far as it feels comfortable. The transition from one sound to the next is rapid, ensuring the air and vowels constantly flow through the imposto.

Back and side of tongue consonants

NGAA NGAA NGAA NGAA NGAA

The sound NGAA is produced both in the imposto with the *n* sound and by the middle of the back of the tongue brought forward to meet the central portion of the back of the hard palate. The middle of the tongue is forward in the mouth, with the soft palate lifted and the fauces stretched. The vowel sound is pure and open. This exercise encourages development of the flexibility of the back of the tongue.

In normal speech level repeat NGAA five times. Singing a descending scale from the C above middle C, repeat NGAA five times on each note ensuring each new tone starts with a clear 'n' sound. Repeat this exercise moving up one semitone, as far as it feels comfortable, and down one semitone, as far as it feels comfortable.

GAA GAA GAA GAA GAA

The sound GAA is produced by the middle of the back of the tongue brought forward to meet the central portion of the hard palate. The middle of the tongue is forward in the mouth, with the soft palate lifted and the fauces stretched. The vowel sound is pure and open. This exercise encourages development of the flexibility of the back of the tongue.

In normal speech level repeat GAA five times. Singing a descending scale from the C above middle C, repeat GAA five times on each note. Repeat this exercise moving up one semitone, as far as it feels comfortable and down one semitone, as far as it feels comfortable.

YAA YAA YAA YAA YAA

The sound YAA is produced by the sides of the tongue against the upper molar teeth, with the soft palate lifted and the fauces stretched. The vowel sound is pure and open. This exercise encourages development of the flexibility of the sides of the tongue.

At normal speech level repeat YAA five times. Singing a descending scale from the C above middle C, repeat YAA five times on each note. Repeat this exercise moving up one semitone, as far as it feels comfortable, and down one semitone, as far as it feels comfortable.

The exercises given in the warm up section p. 59 will allow you to feel where each of the sounds are made and placed.

Appoggio

Appoggio means, 'leaning/support' and is an important part of Bel Canto technique. The breath needs to have somewhere to lean so it can resonate; there are several areas where this can be felt.

Five appoggi areas are given in this book; there are others but their study is beyond the scope of this text.

When singing, the air and vowels are mentally *leant* into the appoggio areas (Figure 17).

The main area, which should always be in use and, in fact, must be connected first, is of course the imposto.

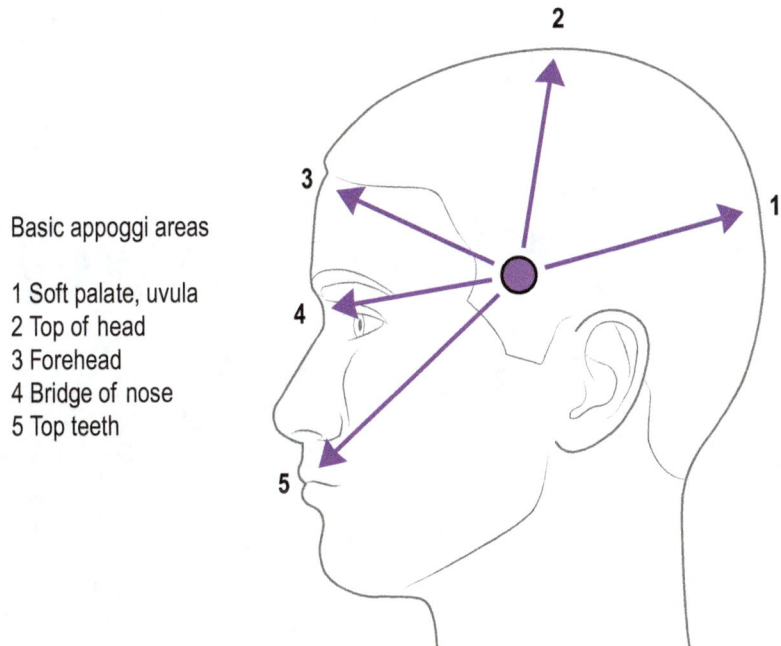

Basic appoggi areas

1 Soft palate, uvula
2 Top of head
3 Forehead
4 Bridge of nose
5 Top teeth

Figure 17: Appoggi areas.

Chapter 4
Understanding how to sing a song

The approach to singing a song to achieve application of the Bel Canto method is a bit more complex than just joining in and singing along to your favourite song. As the sung voice has different qualities to the spoken voice, and as the aim of the Bel Canto technique is to develop your voice so that you can sing, unamplified, in a room or hall, it is necessary to give some attention to how a new song is approached and developed. It is also worth noting that even when you can sing the song, as your muscles develop and your technique improves you will find more opportunities to work on it further and continue to extend the range and timbre of your voice.

Three songs are given here to work on as examples, '*Sebben, crudele*', '*Caro mio ben*', and 'The Sally Gardens'. When studying a new song to sing in Bel Canto technique and attempting to apply all the skills learnt in the warm up exercises, it sometimes feels similar to learning to drive a car, there are so many things to think about at the same time, and when you concentrate on any one skill you forget to do other things you felt were fine. Do not worry, slow improvements will happen each time you practise.

Getting to know the song

1.   *Tempo*
When looking at a new song for the first time, always take time to read the music through, check the time signature and see if it alters at any time throughout the piece, check for any repeated sections and codas. Speak the song out loud in the rhythm written. Both rapidly moving phrases and sustained phases need to be noted. Ensure that when saying the words there is a mental push for each beat and that

minims and semibreves are held for the full count. In '*Sebben, crudele*', and 'The Sally Gardens' the words at the end of the each phrase and verse must be sustained for three beats. If there is a repeated note or a run of notes to be sung on the same vowel, the vowel must be repeated on every note and mentally exaggerated. In 'The Sally Gardens' the vowels are mainly repeated over two notes. In '*Sebben, crudele*' each vowel is mainly on one note with a few on two. Check for dotted beats which are usually followed by a quaver or shorter note. This is seen in 'The Sally Gardens' at the end of phrases one and two over each verse. Checking the tempo and shape of the piece at the outset will make the songs easier to sing, as you will already know how the words fit with the music, and it will also help to make sense of the rhythmic line.

2. Pronunciation

The details of the pronunciation of the three songs are shown. The consonant placing is indicated and the Italian vowel sounds identified. Saying these songs out loud in Bel Canto spoken voice will encourage your flexibility, help you articulate the consonants rapidly and appreciate the vowel sounds you need to sing for each word.

Vowels

The vowels are the parts of words that carry the sound when singing and are vital for achieving clear enunciation. The pronunciation of the Italian vowels is described in Table 1. Thinking about these, read through each phrase of one of the songs out loud, slowly, and in rhythm, using the Italian open vowels. There is no doubt that this will sound quite odd and nothing like you would pronounce words in normal speech. Do not worry if it sounds silly, as this will translate into a good, clear, open sound when singing the song. By identifying which words have the same vowel sounds you can be aware that you do not need to change the position of the soft palate, fauces, or tongue as you move from one to the other. For example, in '*Sebben, crudele*', the word fedele is pronounced feh - deh - leh with no change of vowel; in

'The Sally Gardens', the word 'gardens' will be pronounced, 'gah – dah – ns'. So you only need to flick your tongue to sound the 'd' between the two vowels. When a vowel is articulated on more than one note, such as the first word 'down,' it should be pronounced dah - ahwn, so the 'o' is pronounced AH on the second note as well as the first. This stops the singer from making the N on the second note and singing on a closed sound. In some cases where more than one vowel is sung on the same note the change of vowel must be clear. In *'Caro mio ben'*, at the end of the first line, the sung sound at the end of the word cred*imi* and the beginning of the word *a*lmen is m(ee-ah).

Consonants
It is important that each consonant is clearly and very quickly articulated so the sound moves to the vowel. This will give a legato line when singing and clear diction. Remember there is a different approach for the beginning and ends of words. Before articulating the *'d'* for the first word, 'Down' in 'The Sally Gardens', begin by breathing in and making a short hum. Try imagining the *'d'* in the imposto and the air moving the AH vowel through the forehead. This method will also help place the *'b'* sound in the word 'But' at the end of each verse. To get the end consonants articulated well, speak through each phrase slowly, joining the consonants at the end of each word, with the beginning of the next as appropriate. In the first phrase the *'s'* of 'gardens' moves to the beginning of 'my' as the phrase continues. Where the word is followed by a breath the consonant should be crisply articulated, as in the end of the phrases in Sally Gardens, where 'meet' and 'feet' should have a very clear *'t'* sound at the end.

Interpreting the song

1. *Phrasing and taking a breath*
When approaching a new song, look at the meaning and the composer's phrasing. Look at the places where taking a breath makes

sense both musically and grammatically. Sometimes a singer will need to adjust where to breathe if the phrase is too long, especially in the beginning stages of development, but it is better to breathe than to run out of breath and lose the quality of the sound. However, never breathe in the middle of a word unless it is for interpretation purposes. This means that more time is taken to breathe and a stress is put on the word that follows. This will give the breath, and the space it creates, meaning and will not sound as if the singer has just run out of breath.

2. Dynamics

Dynamics in music are indicated on a score by the composer and add their emotional intentions to the song. All emotional experiences are related to changes in how breath is released. Changes in the movements of the breath are the basis of crying, laughing, sighing, being surprised or shocked, and illustrate why emotion in singing is so very important. The mood of the written dynamics is often supplemented by words in Italian over the score. When reading a score, note the dynamic instructions given and how they relate to the phrasing. All the songs given begin softly. The instructions for '*Caro mio ben*' is *largetto sostenuto*, fairly slowly and sustained and *p sempre*, always soft. In 'The Sally Gardens' the song starts with *sempre p e legato*, always soft and smooth. This later moves to *più f*, a little louder, but the dynamic lines move to a diminuendo (getting softer). Similary '*Sebben, crudele*', although moderately fast and graceful (*allegretto grazioso*), starts softly, *p*, and is louder, *mf*, for the repeat phrase. In the early stages of learning to sing it is difficult to control the volume of the sound produced and follow these instructions. If the singer tries too early to make a *p* or *pp* (soft or very soft) note, there is a danger that the breath flow will slow down too much and the voice will fall out of the imposto and into the throat or back of the nose. Therefore it is better to keep the voice louder by keeping the air flowing faster until a later stage in development. Until that stage, understand the dynamics but interpret them mentally by thinking the voice soft rather than trying to manipulate it.

The musical score will indicate places where the composer feels the words should be stressed by a slightly louder sound. These should be recognized as they are very important and give the feeling of movement and flow. The first beat in the bar is always a stress beat, but other beats may be added. A stress beat is made by moving more air through the vowel rather than making the consonant heavy. When stressing a beat, always emphasize the vowel not the consonant.

3.　*Lyrics and emotional understanding*

Singing is not just about making a beautiful sound. It is about understanding the text and emotion of the piece and communicating it to the audience. Without this, the singer is boring and the audience will quickly lose interest. For this reason, the story within the song must be fully understood so that it can be conveyed to the audience from the soul. If it is a character or operatic aria rather than just a song, then the character must be fully understood and the singer must become that character. It is better to have 90% technique and 100% communication than 100% technique and 90% communication. For all songs in another language it is important to find a translation so the meaning of the words and phases are clear.

Mental application of Bel Canto techniques

A good singer is like a ventriloquist. All the work should be internal with very little or no visual sign externally of the actual effort involved. The only facial expression should be a pleasant smile with a relaxed jaw that does not open too widely when singing open vowels or move too much when forming well-articulated consonants. When everything is in the correct place and the air is flowing freely, the voice will feel more effortless and may suddenly feel disconnected from the body with the sound being larger than expected and some distance in front of your body. It may even feel out of control, which can be unnerving when first experienced. Do not worry, just let it go. This is the beginning stage of freeing the voice and mastering a good technique. Do not worry if the feeling or sound of your voice changes. This will occur as the voice develops and will continue to do so throughout the whole of your singing career.

Singing involves using structures we can never see, so it relies on internal visualization and developing a mental image of what is going on. It would be better if subjective terms for describing singing were replaced by more specific and exact words and language, but even if everyone agreed on the names of the structures used when singing, the sensations and perceptions generated when singing are experienced differently by each singer. To compound this, the feedback of whether the correct thing has been done is evaluated not by your own internal sensations, but by what your teacher and others can hear; their perception of the sound waves generated. Thus the only way we can improve is to link the times the teacher says, 'That's it! Do that again!' with the feeling and thought we had at that time. Thus, until everyone has an image of their internal anatomy and how to control it, each singer will need to create their own mental picture of the structures used and the feelings generated when singing.

Analogies to help imagine parts of the vocal tract

You may find these helpful:

- A large dome lifting the soft palate and uvula up towards the top of the head.
- A little person pushing the soft palate and uvula upwards with his head, his hands pushing the fauces apart and wide, his feet pushing the back of the tongue forward.
- A smiling soft palate and fauces.
- A large AH stretching the soft palate, uvula, and fauces open.
- Laughing in the soft palate.

- Dragon's open nostrils.
- Laser beam flowing through the forehead and between the eyes to show the focused air flow.
- Water fountain through the top of the head with a ping-pong ball on the top – this is the air flow with the sung word flowing on top of it.
- Water blown out through the top of the head like a whale – this is to feel the appoggia area.
- A conveyer belt of flowing air, with the words travelling on it.
- Smooth flowing water stream with leaves gently falling onto it without disturbing the flow – the stream is the free-flowing breath and the leaves are the words flowing on the breath without disturbing the legato line.
- A string of pearls – the string is the breath and the pearls are the words, which are joined together with the string.

The last three on the list are all mental pictures of constant free-flowing air with the words flowing on it.

Chapter 5
Example songs

Three song examples are given to show the singer how to use the Italian vowels and where to place the consonants: *'Sebben, crudele'*, *'Caro mio ben'*, and 'Down by the Sally Gardens'. In each case the tables show the words of the song and the pronunciation you should use when singing. When the songs are sung in this way the audience will hear the words as they are written.

Read through each song using the singing pronunciation shown in the right column of the table. You would normally take a breath at the end of each phrase but, when learning, take a breath at the end of the lines shown. Notice the beginning consonants of the lines shown and see how many can be used to connect the air to the imposto. Notice the end consonants and how they are linked to the beginning of the next word. Now say the words out loud with the singing pronunciation. Smile, feel the soft palate lift, the fauces stretch, and feel the free movement of air through the pharynx and through the soft palate as you say the vowels. It may sound odd but when sung the words will be clear to the audience.

This exercise does take time and practise, but is very important when learning new songs and ensuring you have good placing and pronunciation of songs you have learnt previously.

'Sebben, crudele' by Antonio Caldara (1670–1736).

This song can be found in *Twenty-Four Italian Songs and Arias* published by Schirmir.

Actual words	Sung pronunciation
Sebben, crudele, mi fai languir	S(eh)-bb(eh)-ncr(oo)-de(eh-eh)-l(eh), m(ee)-f(ah-ah)(ee)-l(ah)-ngw(ee-ee)r
sempre fedele, sempre fedele ti volglio amar.	S(eh)-mpr(eh)-f(eh)-d(eh-eh)-l(eh), S(eh)-mpr(eh)-f(eh)-d(eh-eh)-l(eh)-t(ee)-v(oh-oh)-l(ee-oh)-(ah-ah)-m(ah)r.
Repeat above lines x2	
Con la lunghezza del mio servir	C(oh)-nl(ah)-l(oo)-ng(eh)-dz(ah)-d(eh)-lm(ee-oh)-s(eh-eh)-rv(ee)r
la tua fierezza la tua fierezza saprò stancar	L(ah)-t(oo-ah)-f(ee-eh)-r(eh)-dz(ah), l(ah)-t(oo-ah)-f(ee-eh)-r(eh)-dz(ah), s(ah-ah)-pr(oh)-st(ah-ah)-nc(ah)r
la tua fierezza la tua fierezza saprò stancar	L(ah)-t(oo-ah)-f(ee-eh)-r(eh)-dz(ah), l(ah)-t(oo-ah)-f(ee-eh)-r(eh)-dz(ah), s(ah-ah)-pr(oh)-st(ah-ah)-nc(ah)r

Table 3: Pronunciation of 'Sebben, crudele'.

'Caro mio ben' by Giuseppe Giordani (1751–1798)

This song can be found in *Twenty-Four Italian Songs and Arias* published by Schirmir.

Actual words	Sung pronunciation
Caro mio ben credimi almen	C(ah)-r(oh)-m(ee-oh)-b(eh)n, cr(eh)-d(ee)-m(ee-ah)-lm(eh)n
Senza di te languisce il cor	S(eh)-ntz(ah)-d(ee)-t(eh)-l(ah-ah-ah)-ngw(ee)-sh(eh-ee)-lc(oh-oh)r
Caro mio ben,	C(ah)-r(oh)-m(ee-oh)-b(eh)n,
Senza di te languisce il cor	S(eh)-ntz(ah)-d(ee)-t(eh-eh)-l(ah-ah)-ngw(ee-ee)-sh(eh-ee)-lc(oh)r
Il tuo fedel sospira ognor	(Ee)-lt(oo-oh)-f(eh)-d(eh)-ls(oh)-sp(ee)-r(ah-oh)-ny(oh)r
Cessa, crudel, tanto rigor!	Ch(eh)- s(ah)- cr(oo)-d(eh-eh)- lt(ah-ah)-nt(oh-oh)-r(ee-ee)-g(oh)r
Cessa, crudel, tanto rigor, tanto rigor!	Ch(eh)-s(sah)-cr(oo)-d(eh)l-t(ah)-nt(oh)-r(ee)-g(oh)r!
Caro mio ben credimi almen	C(ah)-r(oh)-m(ee-oh)-b(eh)n, cr(eh)-d(ee)-m(ee-ah)-lm(eh)n
Senza di te languisce il cor	S(eh)-ntz(ah)-d(ee)-t(eh)-l(ah-ah-ah)-ngw(ee)-sh(eh-ee)-lc(oh-oh)r
Caro mio ben, credimi almen,	C(ah-ah-ah)-r(oh)-m(ee-oh)-b(eh)n, cr(eh-eh-eh)-d(ee)-lm(ee-ah)-lm(eh)n,
Senza di te languisce il cor	S(eh)-ntz(ah)-d(ee)-t(eh-eh)-l(ah)-ngw(ee)-sh(eh-ee)-lc(oh)r.

Table 4: Pronunciation of 'Caro mio ben'.

'Down by the Sally Gardens' by William Butler Yeats, arranged by Benjamin Britten

Actual words	Sung pronunciation
Verse 1	
Down by the Sally Gardens	Da(h)-(ah)wnb(ah)-yth(ah)-(ah)Sa-lly-(ee)ga(h)-dahns
My love and I did meet,	M(ah)-(ah)ylo-v(ah)-(ah)nd(ah)-di-dm(ee)t,
She passed the Sally Gardens	She-ep(ah)sse-dth(ah)-(ah)Sa-lly-(ee)ga(h)-da(h)ns
With little snow white feet.	Wi-ithli-tt(ah)-(ah)lsn(oh)-w(ah)-tf(ee)t.
She bid me take life easy	She-bi-dm(ee)-(ee)t(eh)-kel(ah)if(ee)-s(ee)
As the leaves grown on the tree,	(Ah)-zth(ah)-l(ee)-vzgr(oh)-w(oh)-(oh)nth(ah)-(ah)tr(ee),
But I was young and foolish	B(ah)-(ah)t(ah)-w(ah)-(ah)zy(ah)-ng(ah)-(ah)ndf(oo)-lish
With her did not agree.	Wi-th-h(ah)-di-dn(ah)-t(ah)-gr(ee).

Table 4: Pronunciation of 'Down by the Sally Gardens'.

Chapter 6
Prepare to sing

The exercises given here are a complete warm-up for the voice before singing. It will take about 20 minutes to complete. Do not use full voice or push your voice to make it loud until you have warmed up.

Check your posture

- Feet – slightly apart
- Knees – loose and not locked
- Back – straight
- Anterior abdominal wall and pelvic floor – relaxed
- Chest – expanded
- Shoulders – rolled backwards, down and relaxed
- Arms – hanging loosely down by your side
- Head and chin – facing straight forward
- Jaw – in relaxed position
- Tongue – forward, flat and relaxed
- Cheeks– -lifted as a small smile

First breaths

- Breathe in through the nose and quickly blow the breath through the lips without vocalizing.
- Do this three times.
- Breathe in through the nose and blow the breath out again, this time vocalizing a WHOOO sound.
- Do this three times.

Sustained breath flow

This is to get you to think consciously about breathing in and out, the movements of your pelvic floor and anterior abdominal wall, and your posture at the end of your breath. The exercise will increase your lung capacity and breath control.

- Breathe in through the nose. As you breathe in your anterior abdominal wall will move out.
- Release the breath slowly making a sissing sound.
- The tip of your tongue should be behind your teeth.
- As you breathe out you should feel some tension in your pelvic floor and lower anterior abdominal wall. This is supporting the breath.
- Sssssss.
- Do this three times making each one last a little longer.

Time how many seconds you can keep the air flowing. Be aware of your pelvic floor muscles, the control and support when breathing.

Blowing air out on the sound WHOOO

- Breathe in through the nose and blow the air out through the lips quickly, on two notes up and down starting on middle C: C-D-C-D-C-D-C.
- Repeat this a semitone higher each time until you reach C above middle C.
- Breathe in through the nose and blow short puffs of air out on each note through the lips, down the scale from the C above middle C. Focus the air as it passes through the upper lip and mentally over the top teeth.
- Repeat this starting a semitone higher each time until you reach upper F or up as far as it feels comfortable.

Glissando on a WHOOO sound

- Breathe in through the nose and blow out through the lips as if gliding up and down the octave.
- Repeat this starting a semitone higher each time until you reach upper F or as far as it feels comfortable.

Finding the imposto

- Breathe in through the nose, then place a finger against one nostril to close it off. Blow the air out through the open nostril making a long HNN sound.
- Breathe in through the nose again, then place a finger against the other nostril to close it off. Blow the air out through the other open nostril making a long HNN sound.
- Repeat this three times with each nostril.
- Breathe in through the nose and blow the air out through both nostrils making the HNN sound.
- Repeat this three times on flowing air. Think of it as blowing your nose repeatedly.

One nostril or one side of your nasal cavity may be more congested than the other, so repeating this exercise on that side will help to clear it.

Humming with singing scales

For all the following exercise, if you are an alto, baritone, or lower, start the following descending exercises on the B above middle C. Sopranos and tenors start on the C above middle C.

- Breathe in through the nose, then place a finger against one nostril to close it off as before. Blow the air through the open nostril and HNN on each note down the octave scale.

- Repeat this starting a semitone higher each time, until you reach upper F.
- Repeat this for the other nostril.

Glissando on a hum HNN

- Breathe in through the nose and glissando HNN through all notes, as if gliding or making a sound like a siren, up and down the octave.
- Repeat this starting a semitone higher each time until you reach upper F or as far as it feels comfortable.

Exercises for tongue flexibility – saying the sounds

- Breathe in through the nose.
- Moving the back of the tongue very fast, make the sounds NGAA, NGAA, NGAA, NGAA, NGAA (say the sound five times rapidly) on the same pitch.
- Breathe in through the nose.
- Repeat with the sound GAA, GAA, GAA, GAA, GAA.
- Breathe in through the nose.
- Repeat with the sound YAA, YAA, YAA, YAA, YAA.

Tongue flexibility – singing the scales

NGAA

- Breathe in through the nose.
- Sing NGAA, NGAA, NGAA, NGAA, NGAA rapidly on each note down the octave starting on the C above middle C and then a semitone higher each time until you reach F or as far as it feels comfortable.

Make sure to keep the vowel open and the tongue forward. If you find you cannot complete the scale on one breath, just take a breath in through the nose and re-place the >NG = sound in the bridge of the nose and finish the scale.

GAA

- Breathe in through the nose.
- Sing GAA, GAA, GAA, GAA, GAA rapidly on each note down the octave starting on the C above middle C.
- Breathe in through the nose.
- Repeat a semitone higher each time until you reach F or as far as it feels comfortable.

YAA

- Breathe in through the nose.
- Sing YAA, YAA, YAA, YAA, YAA rapidly on each note down the octave starting on C above middle C.
- Breathe in through the nose.
- Repeat a semitone higher each time until you reach F or as far as it feels comfortable.

Consonant L

- Breathe in through the nose.
- With the tip of the tongue behind the front top teeth, sing LEE, LAH on each note down the scale starting on C above middle C.
- Repeat a semitone higher each time until you reach F or as far as it feels comfortable .
- Breathe in through the nose
- Sing LAH, LEH, LEE, LOH, LOO on each note down the scale as before.
- Repeat a semitone higher each time until you reach F or as far as it feels comfortable.

Take a breath when you need to. You may find it helpful to rearticulate a HNN at the start before continuing the scale.

Hum and vowels

MEE

- Breathe in through the nose.
- Hum the mmm sound.
- Sing MEE, on each note down the scale starting on C above middle C.
- Repeat a semitone higher each time up to upper F or as far as it feels comfortable.

It may help to imagine a conveyer belt of air with the MEEEE sound continuously moving forward from the bridge of the nose with just your lips moving to make the m sound as the pitch changes. Nothing else should move. You should visualize the air going upwards and forwards when you sing. The sound may feel as if it is behind your eyes and above your ears.

MEE, MAH

- Breathe in through the nose.
- Sing MEE, MAH on each note down the scale starting on the C above middle C.
- Repeat a semitone higher each time up to upper F or as far as it feels comfortable

MAH, MEH, MEE, MOH, MOO

- Breathe in through the nose.
- Sing MAH, MEH, MEE, MOH, MOO on each note down the scale starting on the C above middle C.
- Repeat a semitone higher each time up to upper F or as far as it feels comfortable.

Use the lips to hum and get the mmm sound in the imposto. Make sure to keep the tongue flat and forward with the tip of tongue behind the lower teeth. It is likely that you will not be able to complete the scale on one breath. Begin by taking a breath after the first four notes in each scale and then try singing the scale faster in one breath.

Searching for the Imposto

Other exercises to work on outside the warm-up given above to feel the stretch of the soft palate and fauces and to feel the air moving.

The sigh

- Check your posture.
- Relax the jaw.
- Lift your cheeks in a small smile.
- Visualize your soft palate and uvula lifting.
- Breathe in through the nose.
- Breathe out on a sigh sending the air and sound up and over the soft palate.
- Repeat three times.
- Feel the stretch and lift of the uvula, soft palate, and fauces.

The sigh with the breath consonant H

- Breathe in through the nose.
- Breathe out as before on a sigh and make the sound HAAAAA.

The H can be used with 'n' and with 'm'. Although the HN sound more easily focuses the air through the imposto, the HM will bring the air more forward into the mouth giving mainly mouth resonance.

Hum and open throat

- With lips closed, make sure the tongue is flat and relaxed, the jaw is relaxed, the soft palate is stretched up and out, and lift the cheeks as a small smile.
- Breathe in through the nose.
- Visualize the vowel AH and HUNN up and down two notes starting on middle C: C-D-C-D-C.
- Make sure the tongue does not lift up and the soft palate does not drop down.
- When humming the upper notes, visualize the soft palate opening outwards and stretching even more.
- This may feel awkward at first but this helps to keep the throat open.

Recognizing the sensations of singing in the imposto (in the placing)

Resonance in the imposto is best felt with a HNN sound. Resonance at the back of your head is best felt with HNG sound. If you resonate in your mouth with the HM sound you must still use the imposto, best felt with the HNN sound.

When the air is connected and flowing through the imposto you may experience various sensations:

- Vibrations in the forehead.
- Eyes may feel as though they are vibrating.
- Tingling in the top and back of the head.
- If the sound it very powerful and on a high note it can cause the skull to feel as if it is swaying from side to side with a feeling of dizziness.

- The sound is edgy and powerful.
- Much easier than you would expect to produce the singing sound.
- More control over dynamics.

Exercises to feel the resonance areas

Back of head resonance – HNG

- Breathe in through the nose.
- Place the middle of the back of the tongue against the soft palate and make the sound HNG.
- Notice the buzzing feeling at the back of the head.
- This is the back resonance working.

Imposto resonance – HNN

- Breathe in through the nose.
- Place the tip of the tongue against the roof of the mouth where the upper front teeth join the gum.
- Make sure that the back of the tongue is now flat in the mouth.
- This is very important as the forehead resonance cannot be felt if the back of the tongue is lifted!
- Make the sound HNN.
- Notice the buzzing feeling in the forehead.
- This is the imposto working.

Front of face resonance – HMM

- Breathe in through the nose.
- Keep the tongue flat in the mouth and not touching the roof of the mouth at all.
- Make the sound HMM (ensure the tongue is not touching any part of the roof of the mouth the air can be felt in the lips)

- Notice the buzzing feeling in the: lips, mouth, teeth, nose and slightly in the forehead: this is frontal resonance.
- Never use this without the imposto being connected.

Chapter 7
Learning to sing

Adult and young voices

It is very important that young voices are nurtured and never pushed or forced in any way. The vocal system is still developing throughout puberty so only the basics of technique should be taught to prevent any voice strain or damage. When the young male voice starts to break, singing must be monitored carefully. Unfortunately for the male singer there is no way of knowing what the voice will be like once it has fully broken and indeed if there will be a voice at all.

In Bel Canto technique all voices are taught in the same way. The main difference is that the male voice has the falsetto range. This is the top area of the voice where the notes are sung in a high pitch, which sounds like a female vocal range. Those who can sing in the falsetto range can use some of the exercises in this book, starting in the falsetto range and bringing the voice down through into full voice; however, great care must be taken that there is a smooth and even blend of the full voice and falsetto. The countertenor voice is the falsetto, which has been trained and developed into a full voice over several years. This must never be attempted without the guidance of a good vocal teacher who understands this type of voice.

Choosing a singing teacher

This can be difficult if you are looking for your first singing teacher and have no idea what is involved in a singing lesson. If a teacher is recommended, make sure it is not just because the pupil likes him/her, but that he/she can teach well. If possible, listen to pupils of various teachers when they are performing. Find out as much information about the teacher as possible, such as their singing and teaching career, how long have they been teaching, the technique they teach and their pupils' achievements. If the teacher is still performing, try to go and listen to them. It is not a negative point if they do not perfom, as many teachers do not have enough practise time to dedicate to their own voice. Never be afraid to telephone a teacher you are considering and ask questions.

During the first lesson, notice how your throat feels during and at the end of the lesson. Of course, some of the exercises may feel very strange and awkward and muscles can feel tired when beginning singing lessons, but if it is painful, sore or hoarse, then something is not quite right.

Do not be put off if a teacher has not been to Music College or a music conservatoire. In fact, some of the best teachers in vocal technique have not been through this process, but have themselves searched out good independent teachers who have spent many years of their lives researching, training, and perfecting the technique. Also, a good teacher does not have to be a good pianist to be able to teach the voice. Many singers expect the singing teacher to be a wonderful pianist, which is not always the case. Of course, they must be able to read music and at least play the melody line accurately, but it is the job of the teacher to focus on the voice not the piano.

Appendix I

Technical exercises for voice development

Vaccai (includes backing CD).

These exercises were written for Bel Canto singers and use every part of the technique in stages in each short piece. The pieces must always be sung in Italian.

Suggested songs for the teenage and adult beginners developing voice

Most of the songs suggested can be sung in any key and by any voice. When choosing repertoire only sing in English, Latin, and Italian to begin with. German and French are more difficult and need to be learnt with open vowels and correct use of the tongue.

Classical songs

- 'I Attempt from Love's Sickness' ~ Purcell
- 'Silent Worship' ~ Handel
- 'Where'er you Walk' ~ Handel
- 'Linden Lea' ~ Vaughn Williams
- 'Brahms Lullaby' ~ Brahms
- *'Panis Angelicus'* ~ C. Frank (Latin)
- *'Ave Maria'* ~ Schubert (Latin)
- 'Path to the Moon' ~ Eric Thiman

Italian songs (sung in Italian)

- *'Lascia Ch'io Pianga'* ~ Handel
- *'Caro Mio Ben'* ~ Giordani Caldara
- *'Sebben Crudele'* ~ Giordani Caldara

- *'Ombra mai fu'* ~ Handel
- *'Alma del core'* ~ Antonio Caldara
- *'Star Vicino'* ~ Salvator Rosa
- *'Se tu m'ami'* ~ Pergolesi
- *'Vieni, Vieni'* ~ Vivaldi
- *'Per la Gloria'* ~ Bononcini

Folk and traditional songs

- 'The Sally Gardens' ~ arr. Benjamin Britten
- 'The Turtle'Dove' ~ Traditional ~ arr. David Bray
- 'She's Like the Swallow' ~ Traditional ~ arr. Carl Strommen
- 'Shenandoah' ~ Traditional
- 'Santa Lucia' ~ Traditional (sung in Italian or English)
- 'Scarborough Fair' ~ Traditional ~ arr. By Jay Althouse
- 'The Lark in the Clear Air' ~ Traditional

Popular songs

- 'Moon River' ~ Mercer and Mancini
- 'Somewhere over the Rainbow' ~ *Wizard of Oz*
- 'I could have Danced all Night' ~ *My Fair Lady*
- 'I Feel Pretty' ~ *West Side Story*
- 'The Hills are Alive' ~ *Sound of Music*
- 'When I Fall in Love' ~ by Young and Heyman
- 'Be my Love' ~ by Cahn and Brodsky

Appendix II

Singers to listen to who use Bel Canto technique

It is possible to listen to recordings of these singers on the internet. Think about how the air flow feels, how the sound is produced when you are singing, and see if you can hear and recognize how these singers are breathing, using their vocal tracts, and focusing the air at the imposto.

- Claudia Muzio ~ Soprano
- Renata Tebaldi ~ Dramatic Soprano
- Rosa Ponselle ~ Dramatic Soprano
- Dame Eva Turner ~ Dramatic Soprano.
- Victoria de los Angeles ~ Lyric Soprano
- Lucia Popp~ Coloratura Soprano
- Enrico Caruso ~ Dramatic Tenor
- Mario Lanza ~ Dramatic Tenor
- Franco Corelli ~ Dramatic Tenor
- Beniamino Gigli ~ Lyric Tenor
- Jussie Bürling ~ Tenor

Glossary

Anterior abdominal wall. The front of the body between the lower borders of the ribs and the upper edge of the pelvis. It is composed of the rectus abdominis muscle, the internal and extermal oblique and transversalis abdominis muscles.

Appoggio. The word means support. In singing is used to describe the support of the air flow which feels as if it is leaning on various places in the body and head. When breathing in and when breathing out the thorax is open and the air leans against the ribs. When singing vowel sounds they can be felt within the skull. Older books relate appoggio to the vibration of the air as it passes through the glottis.

Arytenoid cartilage. One of a pair of small cartilages found on the posterior surface of the cricoid cartilage. Each has a process for the attachment of muscles which open the glottis and another from which the vocal cord and vocalis muscle extends to the inner aspect of the thyroid cartilage.

Baroque period. Period of time from 16th to early 18th centuries.

Castrato (castrati). A male singer without testes who has not been through the hormonal changes which normally occur at puberty. Their larynx does not enlarge and their voice has the same sound as a young boy. Their lung capacity and breath control is the same as an adult man.

Consonants. The parts of speech which are not vowels, usually made with parts of the tongue or lips.

Conus elasticus. A connective tissue membrane which stretches from the cricoid cartilage to the arytenoid cartilages on each side. The free edge of the conus elasticus vibrates when air passes upwards from the trachea producing sound.

Coronal section. A body plane taken through the head passing through both ears. A coronal section shows all the related structures within the plane.

Cricoid cartilage. A ring of cartilage at the top of the trachea. It articulates with the arytenoid cartilages and the thyroid cartilage.

Diaphragm. A sheet of muscle and connective tissue which separates the thorax from the abdomen. When it descends, the pressure in the thorax lowers and air enters the lungs.

Diphthong. Two vowels sounds on a single syllable. Italian vowels do not have diphtongs.

Dynamics. The change in volume between loud and soft as indicated on a musical score.

Epiglottis. A shoehorn shaped cartilage within the larynx. It normally moves backwards during swallowing, preventing food from entering the larynx and trachea.

Ethmoid sinuses. Clusters of small holes within the ethmoid bones which connect to the nasal cavity.

Facial bones. The bones of the face: frontal, zygomatic, maxillary, mandibular.

False vocal cord. Folds of mucous membrane within the larynx above the true vocal folds, which lead to the ventricle of the larynx.

Fauces. Two folds of mucous membrane each containing muscles passing from the soft palate to the tongue and pharynx. The front is termed the palatoglossal arch; behind is the palatopharyngeal arch. The palatine tonsil can be seen between them on each side. The contained muscles tense and move the palate.

Frontal sinuses. Holes within the frontal bones on each side which connect to the nasal cavity.

Glissando. Movement of sound smoothly from a low to a higher pitch and back down again.

Glottis. The name of the space between the two vocal folds.

Hard palate. The roof of the mouth which separates the oral cavity from the nasal cavity.

Hyoid bone. A small bone found at the front of the neck above the larynx. It provides attachment for muscles of the tongue and the front of the neck.

Imposto. A place between the eyes, just above the bridge of the nose. The term is used to describe where the air flow should feel to be flowing and resonating.

Intercostal muscles. External and internal intercostal muscles connect each rib to the rib below. When they contract the ribs move upwards and outwards, increasing the volume of the thorax and drawing air into the lungs.

Italian vowels. The particular vowels used in Bel Canto singing to produce a clear sound.

Jaw. The mandible and lower teeth.

Laryngopharynx. That part of the pharynx which is directly behind the larynx and particularly the epiglottis.

Laryngoscope. A device which enables someone to see the vocal folds in life and evaluate their movement when talking and singing.

Larynx. A group of cartilages that support the vocal folds and control the entrance to the trachea, so that food and liquid does not pass into the lungs.

'Lean the air'. This phrase is associated with the appoggio areas. It is a feeling which develops as the technique is learnt.

Legato. A smooth singing sound when changing pitch.

Lyrics. The words of a song.

Maxillary sinuses. Holes within the maxillary bones on each side, beneath the orbits, which connect to the nasal cavity.

Mucous membrane. A covering epithelium with an underlying lamina propria enveloping structures within the nasal and oral cavities and the larynx. In the oral cavity, the epithelium is stratified, squamous, non-keratinizing epithelium; in the nasal cavity the epithelium is pseudostratified, ciliated columnar epithelium with goblet cells. The vocal folds within the larynx are covered locally with stratified, squamous, non-keratinizing epithelium.

Nasal cavity. The air space above the hard and soft palates.

Nasopharynx. That part of the pharynx which is directly behind the nasal cavity.

Oropharynx. That part of the pharynx which is directly behind the oral cavity (mouth).

Palate. The bony and muscular structure which separates the oral cavity (mouth) from the nasal cavity.

Pelvic floor. The muscles at the lower end of the trunk which control all excretory functions. Raising the pelvic floor muscles controls the excretory sphincters.

Pharynx. A fibroelastic tube which extends behind the nasal cavity, oral cavity, and larynx and is continuous with the oesophagus.

Phrasing. Indications on music about where breaths should be taken to best interpret the lyrics.

Resonance. The vibration of air in a cavity. In singing, when the resonance of the vocal tract matches the resonance frequency of the room and the amplitude of the heard sound increases.

Sagittal section. A body plane taken through the head passing from the nose to the back of the head. A sagittal section shows all the related structures within the plane.

Soft palate. Muscular structure at the back of the hard palate, composed of mucous membrane and muscles which tense and lift the soft palate.

Sphenoid sinus. A midline hole within the sphenoid bone which connects to the nasal cavity.

Sternum. The bone at the front of the chest which articulates with the ribs.

Tempo. The time signature of a piece of music with instructions to keep to time strictly or slow down in places

Thyroid cartilage. A large cartilage with a midline prominence which characterizes the larynx. It articulates with the cricoid cartilage and is the site of the anterior attachment of the vocal cords and vocalis muscle. It is larger in men than women.

Transverse section. A body plane taken across the long axis or any structure. A transverse section shows all the related structures within the plane.

Uvula. Midline structure of the soft palate.

Vibrato. Small variation of pitch on a sung note. In Bel Canto technique the production of clear Italian vowels produces hardly any vibrato.

Vocal fold. The free edge of the conus elasticus supported by vocalis muscle which vibrates when air from the trachea passes over it.

Vocal fold. Mucous membrane covering the vocalis muscle and the free edge of the conus elasticus which vibrates when air from the trachea passes over it.

Vocalis. Small muscle, part of thyroarytenoid, which extends from the arytenoid cartilage to the thyroid cartilage. It prevents overstretching of the free edge of the conus elasticus.

Vowels. The open sounds produced by the shape of the oral cavity and oropharynx, controlled by the tension and position of the soft palate.

References

Altman, K. W. (2007) Vocal Fold Masses. *Otolaryngol Clin N Am* 40:1091–1108.

Celletti, R. (1991) *A History of Bel Canto.* Oxford: Oxford University Press.

Courey, M., Postma, G.N., Ossoff, R.H. (2010) The Professional Voice. Chapter 61 in Flint, P.W., et al (Eds) *Cummings Otolaryngology* 5th ed.

Deutsch, G., (2011). 8 things you didn't know about Tony Bennett. abc News, September 9, 2011, http://abcnews.go.com/Entertainment/things-tony-bennett/story?id=14473251 (accessed March 2014)

Giles, P. (2006). *A Basic Countertenor Method.* London: Kahn & Averill.

Jenkins, J. S. (2000). The Lost Voice: A History of the Castrato. *Pediatr Endocrinol Metab* 13 Suppl 6:1503–8

Koufman, J. A., Radomski, T. A., Joharii, et al. (1996). Laryngeal biomechanics of the singing voice. *Otolaryngol Head Neck Surg.* 115:527–37.

Mancini, G. (1776). *Practical Reflections on the Figurative Art of Singing.* Richard G Badger (Ed). Boston, MA: The Gorman Press Boston, 1912.

Manén, L. (1974). *The Art of Singing.* London: Faber Music Ltd.

Manén, L. (1977). *Bel Canto. The Teaching of the Classical Italian Songschools, its Decline and Restoration.* Oxford: Oxford University Press

McGovern, D. (2011). *Mario Lanza: A Radical Reassessment.* http://www.mariolanzatenor.com/a-radical-reassessment.html (accessed March 2014).

Miller, R. (1996). *The Structure of Singing. System and Art in Vocal Technique*. Schirmer. Thompson Learning.

Morris, C. (2010). *Making it look easy: The Art of Frank Sinatra*. http://www.sinatra.com/legacy/making-it-look-easy (accessed March 2014).

Okutman, T. (2008). http://www.timurokutman.com/en/farinelli.htm (accessed March 2014)

Stark, J. A. (1938) *Bel Canto: A History of Vocal Pedagogy*. Toronto: University of Toronto Press

Yiu, E. M. L., Chen, F. C., Lo, G., Pang, G. (2012). Vibratory and perceptual measurement of resonant voice. *J Voice* 26:675. e13–19

Index

air sinuses 6, 9, 29, 30, 31
anterior abdominal wall 9, 10, 12, 13, 59, 60, 75
appoggio 45, 75, 77
arytenoid cartilage 17, 18, 19, 22, 75, 76

Baroque period 1, 75
breathing 2, 5, 11, 12, 13, 14, 15, 17, 35, 49, 60, 73, 75

castrati 1–3, 75
consonants 5, 24, 40, 41, 42, 43, 48, 49, 51, 55, 56, 58, 65, 75
conus elasticus 18, 19, 20, 22, 75, 79, 80
cricoid cartilage 17, 19, 22, 75, 76, 79
cricothyroid ligament 20

diaphragm 9, 11, 12, 76
diphthong 37, 40, 76
dynamics 32, 50, 67, 76

epiglottis 17, 23, 76, 77
ethmoidal sinuses 30
ethmoid sinuses 76

false vocal folds 17, 76
fauces 26, 27, 28, 29, 37, 38, 40, 42, 43, 44, 48, 52, 55, 65, 76
frontal sinuses 30, 33, 43, 76

glissando 34, 61, 62, 77
glottis 19, 22, 75, 77

hard palate 15, 26, 31, 39, 43, 44, 77, 79
harmonics 6, 13
humming 33, 34, 41, 42, 49, 61, 62, 64, 65, 66
hyoid bone 17, 24, 77

imposto 29, 30, 31, 32, 33, 41, 42, 43, 45, 49, 50, 55, 61, 65, 66, 67, 68, 73, 77
intercostal muscles 11, 77

larynx 4, 6, 11, 17, 18, 19, 20, 23, 30, 75, 76, 77, 78, 79
lateral cricoarytenoid muscle 21
legato 13, 16, 49, 50, 53, 78
lungs 9, 10, 11, 12, 13, 16, 17, 29, 76, 77
lyrics 40, 51, 78

maxillary sinuses 30, 32, 78
mucous membrane 17, 19, 20, 21, 22, 76, 78, 79, 80

nasal cavity 6, 13, 23, 26, 29, 30, 31, 33, 39, 43, 61, 76, 77, 78, 79
nasopharynx 78

oropharynx 78

palate 15, 17, 23, 24, 26, 27, 28, 29, 30, 31, 32, 33, 37, 38, 39, 40, 41, 42, 43, 44, 48, 52, 55, 65, 66, 67, 76, 77, 78, 79, 80
pelvic floor muscles 13, 14, 60, 78
pharynx 6, 14, 17, 23, 24, 26, 27, 28, 29, 30, 31, 33, 37, 38, 42, 43, 55, 76, 77, 78
phrasing 49, 50, 78
posterior cricoarytenoid muscle 21
posture 5, 10, 59, 60, 65
pronunciation 4, 5, 37, 38, 40, 48, 55, 56, 58

resonance 6, 7, 13, 29, 30, 32, 42, 65, 66, 67, 68, 79
ribs 10, 11, 12, 13, 14, 16, 75, 77, 79

shoulders 10, 13, 17
sigh 33, 65
soft palate 17, 23, 26, 27, 28, 29, 30, 33, 37, 38, 39, 40, 41, 42, 43, 48, 52, 55, 65, 66, 67, 76, 79, 80

sphenoid sinus 30, 79

tempo 47, 48, 79
thorax 10, 12, 75, 76, 77
thyroid cartilage 17, 20, 22, 75, 76, 79, 80
tongue 10, 11, 14, 16, 17, 23, 24, 25, 26, 27, 28, 29, 33, 34, 38, 41, 42, 43, 44, 49, 52, 60, 62, 63, 65, 66, 67, 71, 75, 76, 77
trachea 19, 77

uvula 17, 26, 27, 28, 29, 33, 38, 52, 65, 79

vibration 5, 21, 32, 34, 75, 79
vibrato 79
vocal fold 79, 80
vocal folds 3, 4, 6, 11, 17, 18, 19, 20, 22, 76, 77, 78
vocalis 18, 19, 20, 75, 79, 80
vocal ligament 20
vowels 37, 48, 80
    Italian 5, 37, 38, 40, 48, 55, 76, 77, 79

www.ingramcontent.com/pod-product-compliance
Lightning Source LLC
Chambersburg PA
CBHW051104230426
43667CB00013B/2432